TALES OF PERSIA

TALES OF PERSIA

MISSIONARY STORIES FROM ISLAMIC IRAN

WILLIAM McELWEE MILLER

ILLUSTRATED BY BRUCE VAN PATTER

P&R

PUBLISHING

P.O. BOX 817 • PHILLIPSBURG • NEW JERSEY 08865-0817

Page design and typesetting by Lakeside Design Plus

Printed in the United States of America

Library of Congress Cataloging-in-Publication Data

Miller, William McElwee.
    Tales of Persia : missionary stories from Islamic Iran / William McElwee Miller ; illustrated by Bruce Van Patter.
       p. cm.
    ISBN 0-87552-615-2 (pbk.)
    1. Missionary stories. 2 Missions—Iran—Juvenile literature. 3. Missionaries. I. Van Patter, Bruce. II. Title.

BV2087.M475 2005
266'.00955—dc22

2004063193

Dedicated to my grandchildren and to their grandmother,
who served Christ with me in Iran.

Mid–20th Century Iran

Modern–day Iran

Contents

CONTENTS

INTRODUCTION:
WHY I WENT AS
A MISSIONARY TO IRAN

I am an American. I was born in Kentucky, and when I was a boy I lived in Virginia. But I spent many years of my life far from my native land. For forty-three years I was a missionary to Persia, now known by its ancient name, Iran,[1] a country some eight thousand miles east of Virginia. How did this happen, and how am I now able to write for you a book of stories about people in Iran? Let me tell you.

In the Valley of Virginia, about ten miles from the town of Lexington, there is a Presbyterian church named Bethesda. My grandfather and, after him, my father were for many years pastors of that country church. I lived in the manse, the home of

1. Iran is pronounced Er-rahn.

the pastor, with my parents and my brother, Francis, and our little dog, Trigg. We loved the beautiful mountains called Jump and Hogback, which we could see when we played in the yard. We loved our home, where our mother taught us our lessons (we never went to school) and read stories to us. We loved *Tales of a Grandfather* by Sir Walter Scott, which told us about our Scottish heroes. We loved to take care of the garden and the chickens and the horse and the cow and the pigs. And we loved our church, where we worshiped God, and where in Sunday school we recited the many Bible verses and the catechism that we had learned by heart.

We also belonged to a missionary society for the young people and the children of the church that my mother started, called the Kemper Band. It was named for a missionary friend of my mother's, Miss Kemper, who was serving Christ in Brazil. All the members of the Kemper Band gave two cents each week to help Miss Kemper in her missionary work. To earn this money, we used to sell eggs and do chores, for we didn't have much money in those days. We read books about missionaries, and sometimes missionaries came to visit us and speak in our church. Once Miss Kemper herself came. A great missionary from the Congo (Zaire) in Africa named Dr. William Morrison once visited us and told us stories about Africa. How we loved his stories!

When I was still a little boy, I did an important thing: I gave my heart to Jesus Christ. I loved Jesus because he first loved me, and I wanted to serve him. I thought the best way to serve him would to become a minister like my father and both of my grandfathers. But *where* should I serve Christ as a minister? When I heard from the missionaries that there were many people in the world who had never heard of Jesus Christ and his love, I began to wonder whether God might not want me to go to some other country to tell the people the good news that Jesus had come to save them from their sins and to make them children of God. I was willing to do this if God wanted me to, so I waited for him to tell me what to do.

After I had been graduated from college, I went to a big missionary meeting for students in Kansas City, and there I saw many missionaries and heard their addresses. They reminded us that Jesus had commanded his followers to go into all the world and to tell people about him, that they might believe on him. But now, after nineteen hundred years, there were millions of people in many lands who had never seen a Bible or heard the story of Jesus and his love for all the people of the world. And these missionaries asked us students if we should obey Christ and go to a land where most of the people did not know him, and there help to make him known. It seemed to me that this was God's message to me, and after this meeting I decided that, if God permitted me, I would become a missionary in some foreign land. I would try to go, and I thought God would stop me if he did not want me to go abroad. But God did not stop me, so I became a foreign missionary. But when I was in Kansas City, I wasn't yet ready to become a missionary. First, I had to study in a theological seminary to learn more about the Bible and Christian teaching, so that I could teach other people the truth about Jesus Christ.

One of the great missionaries whom I saw in Kansas City and whom I got to know well when I was studying in seminary was Dr. Samuel Zwemer. He had gone to Arabia to tell the people there about Christ. He told us that most of the people of Arabia were Muslims; that is, they were followers of Muhammad, a man who had lived in Arabia about six hundred years after the time of Christ and who had claimed that he was a prophet sent by God. He wanted all the people of the world to believe on him. After his death, his followers conquered many lands with the sword and converted many people to this new religion, which was called Islam. Dr. Zwemer also told us that there were very few missionaries working in Muslim countries, and very few Muslims had ever become Christians. When I heard this, I thought, "Surely some of us students in the seminary should go to the Muslims and tell them of Christ's love for them! Why shouldn't *I* go?" So I decided to become a missionary to Muslims.

But to what land should I go? Muslims live in many countries, and one seventh of the people of the world follow the religion of Islam. Someone suggested to me that I think of going to Persia, the country now known by its old name, Iran. So I read reports on what missionaries were doing in Persia. I learned that Presbyterian missionaries from America had been living and working in that land since 1835, and Episcopal missionaries from England, since 1869. They had hospitals and schools in a number of cities, and some little churches had been established.

I also learned that a new mission station, or center, had been established in the city of Meshed in eastern Iran, the only place in a vast region one thousand miles across where the message of Christ was being given and the love of Christ was being shown to people. (If you look at the map in this book, you will see that this region includes part of Iran, all of Afghanistan, and all of Turkestan.) I felt that God wanted me to go to that greatly neglected part of the world, so I asked the Board of Foreign Missions of the Presbyterian Church to send me to Meshed. How happy I was when, in 1919, I set out from New York on a ship called the *Black Arrow* with eight other missionaries and a little one-year-old missionary boy named Jack—all bound for Iran!

When I reached Teheran, the capital of Iran, I began to learn the beautiful Persian language—for, of course, I could not tell the good news of Christ to the people until I could speak their language and understand what they said to me. After seven months I went on eastward to Meshed, traveling the 560 miles in a wagon drawn by four horses. There were no trains and very few cars in that part of Iran at that time, and there were no good roads. In Meshed, I joined six other missionaries who were treating many sick people in the mission hospital and telling the message of Christ to all who would listen. I was present when the first little group of Muslim men was baptized and became Christians.

I had a Muslim teacher who helped me learn the Persian language well. He also told me a great deal about the religion and customs of the Muslims. In chapter 1, I will tell you a little of what he and others told me, and I will also tell you a little of what I later learned from the books I read about the beliefs of the Muslims of Iran.[2]

BIBLE READING: MATTHEW 28:18–20

2. An account of the history and doctrines and practices of Islam is given in William M. Miller, *A Christian's Response to Islam* (Phillipsburg, N.J.: P&R, 1976).

1

THE STORY OF
MUHAMMAD AND
THE RELIGION OF ISLAM

You remember that I promised to tell you about the religion of the Muslims and about their prophet Muhammad. It is a most interesting story. Muhammad was born in A.D. 570, in the city of Mecca in Arabia. Most of the people of Arabia at that time worshiped idols, and there was a famous idol temple in Mecca. They knew that there was a great God, whom they called *Allah,* but few of the Arabians worshiped him. When Muhammad was a young man, he met some Jews and Christians who did not worship idols but were worshipers of the unseen God. Then, when he was forty years of age, he thought he saw an angel who told him that Allah had appointed him to be a prophet and that he must tell the people to worship only Allah, not idols. So Muhammad began to

 preach. He told the Arabs that one day Allah would raise all the dead people to life. He would take all who had worshiped him and done good deeds to heaven, and he would send those who did not worship him to hell.

A few people believed in Muhammad, but most of the people of Mecca would not listen to him. However, he continued to preach for thirteen years in Mecca. Finally, there was so much opposition to him and his preaching against the idols that Muhammad and his followers left Mecca in A.D. 622. They went to Medina, another city in Arabia, about two hundred miles north of Mecca. There the people received Muhammad and made him their chief, and many believed him to be the prophet of Allah. Before long he began to fight with his enemies in Mecca, and he defeated them. At last he was able to capture their city. When he entered Mecca without a battle, he threw out the idols from the idol temple and made it the center of the religion of Islam.

After that, most of the people of Arabia quickly submitted to Muhammad, and he became their political and their religious ruler. His followers were called *Muslims,* because in the Arabic language the word *muslim* means "one who submits," and they had submitted to Muhammad and to Allah, who they believed had sent Muhammad. After the death of Muhammad in A.D. 632, the Muslim armies soon conquered most of the nearby countries. Later this religion spread westward to Spain, eastward to India, and southward to Africa.

Now let me tell you what the Muslims believe. They believe that God, whom they call Allah, is the one true God who made all things and who has all knowledge and power. He made man to obey and serve him; and when people disobeyed, he sent prophets to tell them what to do and what not to do. Muslims think that there were many prophets, perhaps 124,000 of them, but they do not know the names of most of them. They say that there were five very great prophets: Noah, Abraham, Moses, Jesus, and Muhammad. They believe that Muhammad is the last and the greatest of God's prophets. They think that God gave books to each of the great prophets, as well as to some other prophets. They call the book that they say was given to Jesus *Injil*. They believe that God sent messages in the Arabic language to Muhammad by the angel Gabriel. Muhammad told the people these messages, which were written down by those who heard them. Later they were collected in a book called the *Koran*. Muslims believe that the Koran is the very Word of God and that it should be read in the Arabic language.

What do Muslims know about Jesus Christ? The Koran says that Jesus was a very great prophet, born of the Virgin Mary, but that he was not the Son of God. It also says that Jesus performed wonderful miracles, that he healed the sick people and even raised the dead to life. But it says that he did not die on the cross, for God performed a miracle to save Jesus from death. They say that God changed one of Jesus' enemies to look like Jesus and that this man was crucified in place of Jesus. Then, they say, God took Jesus to heaven, where he is now. They believe that Jesus is alive and that he

will come to earth again and will punish all who do not accept Muhammad. So you see that though Muslims think highly of our Savior Jesus Christ, they do not really know him. They do not know that he is the Son of God and that he loved us so much that he died on the cross to save us from sin and that he rose from the grave alive. They wrongly think that Muhammad took the place of Jesus. They say that people no longer need Jesus and his teachings—all must now submit to Muhammad and the Koran.

Muslims believe that there will be a day of resurrection, when God will raise all the dead people to life, judge them, and send some of them to heaven and some to hell. If people want to get to heaven, they must do certain things. First, they must say the creed of Islam, which is "There is no god except Allah; Muhammad is Allah's Messenger." Then they must worship Allah every day. To do this, they must put some water on their hands and feet, stand facing the city of Mecca, and recite some Arabic sentences. As they do this, they must bow, kneel, touch their foreheads to the ground, rise again, and repeat this ritual several times. This must be done early in the morning, at noon, and in the evening. Many Muslims perform these acts of worship five times each day.

Muslims must also keep the fast of Ramadan. From the time when they first see the new moon in the Muslim month of Ramadan to the next new moon, about twenty-nine days, they are not permitted to eat any food or taste any drink from daylight in the morning till after sunset at night. But all during the night they are allowed to eat and drink. It is hard for working people to keep the fast, especially in hot weather. Muslims also must give money to poor people. Some give pennies to beggars, and others sometimes give large sums for hospitals or schools.

Once in his life, every Muslim who has the money should make the pilgrimage to Mecca. Those who do this gain the title of *Hajji*. Many people in Iran who can't go all the way to Mecca make pilgrimages to Meshed or other cities in which the tombs of descendants of Muhammad are located. Since the followers of the religion of Islam do not have a savior, they hope that by making pilgrimages and doing the other things I have told you about they may please God and get him to forgive their sins and take them to heaven when they die. But they are never sure whether they will go to heaven or to hell when they die.

Many of the Muslim people in Iran were very kind to me. I love them, and I long for them to know and love the Savior Jesus Christ, who died to save them. While I was in Iran, I was happy to know devoted Christians who had been Muslims. The stories of some of these Christians have been told in *Ten Muslims Meet Christ*.[1] But in this little book I want to tell my grandchildren, and other children who love Jesus, some stories about other people in Iran and about interesting experiences I had there. In several stories the names I give to my Iranian friends are not their real names.

Remember that I first went to Iran many years ago, and the conditions in that country as described in some of my stories were then very different from what they are now. Today fine highways have been built, and one can travel all over Iran by bus, train, or plane. Iran has become one of the great oil-

1. William M. Miller, *Ten Muslims Meet Christ* (Grand Rapids: Eerdmans, 1969).

producing countries of the world. In the big cities there are supermarkets and huge apartment buildings. The government has established schools and colleges and hospitals and factories, and many people own cars and radios and televisions. In material things, Iran has made amazing progress since I arrived in that land in 1919. But, sad to say, most of the people do not yet know the love and truth of Jesus Christ.

BIBLE READING: ROMANS 10:1—4

2

A Pioneer Missionary in the Land of the Sun

We all admire pioneers, the brave men and women who explore unknown lands to discover where the rivers come from or where gold or oil or other valuable things are to be found. Some pioneers have even gone to explore the moon. We love to read the stories of their adventures, and we remember their names.

Now I want to tell you the story of a brave pioneer who traveled far not to find gold but to tell people the good news of Jesus Christ. His name was Lewis Esselstyn. He was an American who went to Iran in 1887 as a missionary and lived there for about thirty years. At first his home was in Teheran, the capital of Iran, which you can find on the map. But he often made journeys to other towns in order to know the people and talk to them about his Savior. Once, in the town of Semnan, a Muslim preacher who was a friend of Mr. Esselstyn invited him to preach a sermon in the mosque, the building in which Muslims gather to say their prayers. That is the only time that a Christian missionary has been invited to speak in a mosque in Iran.

When you look at the map of Iran, you will see that east of Teheran, in the northeast corner of the country, is a city called Meshed. It does not seem to be far from the capital, but Meshed is more than five hundred miles from Teheran. Mr. Esselstyn used to think much about this vast region to the east, called *Khorasan* (Land of the Sun), where there were millions of people who did not know and love Jesus Christ. He remembered that Jesus had commanded his followers to tell the good news of salvation to everybody in all parts of the world, and he felt that someone should go to the Land of the Sun to give to the people there the message of Christ, who is the Light of the world. At last he was sure that God wanted *him* to go to Meshed as a pioneer missionary. So he went.

At that time there were no trains or buses running between Teheran and Meshed, and the dirt road was hardly good enough for a horse-drawn wagon. So Mr. Esselstyn rode a horse all this long distance, and it took him a whole month to reach Meshed. How glad he was when at last he saw the city from a distance, and how earnestly he prayed that God would help him to serve Christ well in that place!

Meshed is a special sort of city. Long ago one of the descendants of Muhammad died and was buried there. His name was the Imam Reza. The people thought his enemies had poisoned him, so they said he was a martyr, which is a person who dies for his faith. His friends often visited his grave and wept when they remembered his sufferings, and some of them built houses for themselves near his grave. Thus a town gradually grew up called *Meshed,* which means "place of martyrdom." By degrees this town became a large city. Later a beautiful big tomb was built over the grave of the Imam Reza, with a large golden dome that could be seen from afar as it glittered in the sunshine.

For more than a thousand years, Muslims from all parts of Iran and also from foreign lands have been coming to Meshed on pilgrimages to visit the tomb of the Imam Reza. They say prayers and shed tears over his grave, hoping that God will be pleased with them for making this journey and will forgive their sins. You see, they do not know that Jesus died for us sinners and that all who believe in him will be forgiven by God. Nor do they understand that pilgrimages like this, or other things that we do, will not save us from our sins. From what I have now told you, I am sure you realize that Meshed is a holy city for the Muslims.

Many of the people there were so devoted to their religion that they did not want any Jew or Christian to enter Meshed. What courage it took for Mr. Esselstyn to go to Meshed! Soon he realized the danger, for a few people who could tell by his foreign clothes and his features that he was not a Muslim ran together to attack him. They thought that if a man like this who did not believe in Muhammad entered Meshed, their holy city would be made unclean. The mob of angry men might have killed the missionary, but a friendly man pulled him into the post office and locked the doors so that the crowd could not get in. Then, during the night, he led Mr. Esselstyn out and sent him on his way back to Teheran. How sad the brave pioneer must have been that his effort to serve God in Meshed had failed!

Did Mr. Esselstyn give up his plan to open a Christian mission station in Meshed? Not at all! When real pioneers fail, they

don't give up—they try, try again! So in 1911 back to Meshed
went the missionary. He had grown older and perhaps wiser.
All the hair had fallen off the top of his head, and on his face
had appeared a beautiful red beard. When he left Teheran, he
took with him on the backs of mules many boxes filled with
Bibles and portions of the Bible in the Persian language, and
he hoped that he could remain in Meshed as a bookseller. He
was determined to be careful not to attract crowds or do or say
anything that would cause the people to throw him out of the
city. And this time he was able to remain.

Mr. Esselstyn did not open a bookstore in the bazaar in which
to sell his Bibles. Instead, he went quietly about the city, talking
in a friendly way with the shopkeepers and others whom he
met. Since he spoke the Persian language very well and had a
fine sense of humor, people enjoyed chatting with this foreigner
with the long red beard, and he made many friends in Meshed.
When any men showed interest in his books, he would let them
have copies of the Psalms of David, the gospel of Matthew, or
even the whole New Testament, which Muslims call *Injil*. As I
told you, Muslims believe that God gave books to some of the
prophets, but they do not have these books. Some of them
received Mr. Esselstyn's books gladly and kissed them to show
their respect for God's Word. The missionary also made many
journeys to towns in other parts of Khorasan and gave many
people copies of his books, and they long remembered the man
who spoke Persian so well and who had a long red beard.

Once when several people had gathered about the missionary in the street and were gladly receiving his books, some of
the *mullas* (Muslim teachers) saw them and came to them in
great anger. They shouted at the people, "Don't take those books!

They give wrong teaching, which is against the teaching of our holy book the Koran. Throw those books away at once!"

The people were frightened, but Mr. Esselstyn was not. He smiled, looked at the angry mullas, and said to the people, "My friends, you decide who is right: your mullas or I. They have dyed their beards red with henna because it is said that their prophet Muhammad had a red beard and they want to be like him. But I did not need to dye my beard, for God made it red. And if your mullas should take off their big turbans from their heads, you would see that they have shaved all the hair off their heads. They say that Muhammad used to shave his head, and they want to be like him. But I did not need to shave my head, for see what God has done for me!" With that he took off his hat and showed them his bald head. All the people laughed, and the mullas went away in confusion. So, with courage and ready wit, Mr. Esselstyn was able to carry on his work for Christ in Meshed.

In 1916 a fine young medical doctor named Rolla Hoffman came to Meshed and opened a mission hospital. Crowds of sick people came every day to see him, in hope that he would be able to cure them, for at that time there was no good hospital in Meshed. Mr. Esselstyn helped the doctor manage the hundreds of poor people who crowded about his little office, and he often talked to them about Jesus, who healed the sick. He also gave his books to those who could read—at that time many people in Iran did not know how to read. The Christian doctor became famous in all that region, and more sick people than he was able to care for came to him for treatment.

All was going well for the two missionaries. Then a famine came to the Land of the Sun. No rain or snow fell for a whole year, and the wheat that had been planted in the ground did not sprout and grow. So there was no harvest that summer, and bread became very scarce and very expensive. Since bread is the principal food of many people in Iran, those who had no bread died of starvation.

Also, many people became sick with a bad disease called typhus. The two missionaries did all they could to help the sick people. Mr. Esselstyn was able to get some money from his friends in Iran and in America, and with this he bought bread. He had a cook make a big pot of soup each day. Then he went out to the hungry people and gave each one a little bread and a bowl of soup. Some of the poor people had typhus, and both missionaries got the disease and became very ill. Dr. Hoffman recovered, and after a long rest he was able to carry on his wonderful work as a medical missionary in Meshed. But Mr. Esselstyn did not get well. He died in 1918, and he was buried in Meshed.

On top of the grave of this pioneer missionary a flat stone was placed, and on the stone these words of Jesus were engraved: "Greater love has no man than this, that a man lay down his life for his friends." Truly Mr. Esselstyn had given his life that the people of Khorasan might know Christ and have everlasting life by believing in him. He baptized only one man in Meshed, but after Mr. Esselstyn's death a little church of believers in Christ was formed and is still there today. However, there are still millions of people in that region who have not yet heard the good news of salvation. There is still need for pioneers like Mr. Esselstyn and Dr. Hoffman to go tell them about Christ and show them Christ's love, as did those two faithful missionaries.

BIBLE READING: JOHN 3:14—17; 15:13

3

MORE CHEESE, PLEASE, IN A PAGE OF THAT BOOK!

Gasem had to work hard to get enough money to buy food and clothes for his family. Early every morning he went to his little shop in the bazaar in the city of Meshed, and often he worked there till late at night. In the hot summer days in Iran, many people like to wear light and cool shoes called *giveh,* and in his shop Gasem made the soles for these shoes. He didn't get much money for the soles, but by hard work he was able to make a modest living.

One day when he heard the boom of the cannon, which told the people that it was noon, Gasem closed the door of his shop, locked it carefully, and started toward his home for lunch. On the way he stopped at the bakery to buy some bread for his family. You have seen different kinds of bread, but did you ever see pebble bread? That was the kind of bread Gasem took home with him.

This bread is called pebble bread (in Persian it is *sangac*) because, unlike the bread you eat, it is baked not in an oven but on a big bed of pebbles! Dry fuel is first piled on the pebbles and set on fire, and the little stones become very hot. Then the ashes are brushed off the pebbles, and on them is thrown a slab of dough as big as a bath towel and half an inch thick. When one side is baked, it is turned over with a sort of wooden shovel and baked on the other side. Then it is pulled off the pebbles and hung on a nail in the wall to cool. Little stones that have stuck to the bread are brushed off on the ground and then gathered up to be used again. Pebble bread is made of whole-wheat flour, and when it is hot, it is really delicious. It is also nourishing. Many of the people in Iran eat this kind of bread morning, noon, and night. People too poor to buy meat or other foods live chiefly on bread.

At the bakery, Gasem bought a big slab of *sangac,* rolled it up, and went on to the grocery shop. He said to the grocer, "Give me five rials worth of cheese." The grocer took his knife and cut off a piece of white cheese made from the milk of goats, wrapped it in a piece of paper that he tore from a book behind the counter, and handed it to Gasem. Then Gasem hastened to his little home with his bread and cheese. It had been a long time since he had had his breakfast of bread and cheese and tea, and he was ready for his lunch. When he arrived, the samovar was boiling, and his wife poured water from it on the tea leaves in the teapot. Then she spread a clean cloth on the floor. She put the cheese on a plate and set it on the cloth. Then she broke the slab of bread into pieces and laid them also on the cloth. Then the family sat down on the floor around the cloth to eat their lunch together. At that time many people in Iran did not use chairs or tables but preferred to sit in their stocking feet on their nice carpets.

When Gasem had eaten as much bread and cheese as he wanted and had drunk three little glasses of tea, his eye fell on the piece of paper lying on the floor in which the cheese had been wrapped. He saw that there was something printed on it in his own Persian language, so he picked it up. There were many people in Iran in those days who could not read, for schools were few and most boys and girls had no opportunities to get an education. But Gasem could read well. And since books and papers were scarce, he eagerly began to read aloud to his family what was printed on the piece of paper. It was a story, and it was very interesting.

What Gasem read was something like this: There was once a man who had vineyard, which is a place where grapevines grow. The owner wanted to find some men to work in his vineyard, digging about the roots of the vines and cutting off and burning the branches that had no fruit. So early one morning he went to the square in the center of the village where people often gathered, and there he saw several men waiting for someone to hire them. "Go, work in my vineyard," he said to them, "and I will give you a denar at sunset." That was the right pay for a day's work, so the men agreed and went off to the vineyard to begin their work, and the owner went back to his home. But several times during the day he returned to the square, and each time he saw men standing there, hoping that someone would give them a job. And each time he said to them,

"Go, work in my vineyard, and I will pay you what is right." Late in the afternoon he found some men standing idle in the square, and he sent them also to work in the vineyard.

Finally, at sunset the owner went to the vineyard to pay the workers. He wanted to surprise them, so he told his assistant to call first those who had come last and give to each of them a denar, a whole day's wage. When these men received a denar for one hour's work, they were very happy. And so were those who got a denar for three hours or six hours of work. But when the men who had worked for twelve hours came forward for their pay, they thought they would get more than a denar. But they also were given a denar. So they became angry and complained, saying, "We have worked all through a long hot day, and you are giving us just what you gave the men who worked only one hour!"

To them the owner replied, "Didn't you agree to work all day for a denar? If I want to be generous and give as much to these other men as I gave to you, why are you unhappy? Can't I do what I want with my money?" So he paid them and sent them all away.

When Gasem finished reading this story to his family, he said, "That is very interesting. How generous that man was! I wish I could read other stories like that."

The next day when the noon cannon went off, Gasem closed his shop, went to the bakery and bought a slab of *sangac,* and then went to the grocery store. "Give me five rials worth of cheese," he said to the grocer, "and please wrap it in a page of that book you have behind the counter." So the grocer cut off a piece of cheese, tore another page from the book, wrapped the cheese in it, and gave it to Gasem, who hurried home for

his lunch. Just as soon as he had eaten his bread and cheese and drunk his three cups of tea, he picked up the page from the book and read what was printed on it. This story also was very good. He *must* have more of this book!

On the third day at noon, Gasem once more bought his bread and cheese, and again he asked the grocer to wrap the cheese in another page from the book. "You seem to like that book," said the grocer. "If you give me five more rials, you can have all that is left of it." Gasem gladly paid the price of the cheese and the book, took both home with him, and proudly showed his book to the family. What was this book that had such interesting stories in it? It was the New Testament in the Persian language, and the story about the workers in the vine-yard is from the gospel of Matthew (Matt. 20:1–16). You can find it in your Bible and read it for yourself.

Gasem had often heard that God had given to Jesus a book called the *Injil,* but he had never seen a copy of this holy book. In Iran at that time, Bibles were not as plentiful as they are in our country today, and so very few people had ever had an opportunity to read God's Word. Therefore Gasem was delighted to have a copy of the *Injil* of Jesus, even though the grocer had torn out part of it.

Gasem had an older brother named Muhammad, and as soon as he was able, he took the book to his brother. "Look," he said, "I have a copy of the holy *Injil!*" His brother also was happy to see the precious book. Then Gasem said to Muhammad, "Where do you think this book came from?"

"I don't know," replied his brother, "but probably the grocer got it from that American missionary who came here several years ago. You remember him—the man with the long beard."

"Yes," said Gasem, "but, sad to say, that man died in the famine. Everybody in Meshed knew and thought highly of him for all his kindness to the poor people. If he were alive, we could go to him and perhaps get a book that had not been torn."

"But I have seen another American missionary here," replied Muhammad. "He lives near the American hospital. Let us go to visit him."

So one day the two brothers went to the home of Mr. Donaldson, knocked on the door, and asked to see him. Mr. Donaldson came to the door and gave them a warm welcome. Then they told him about the book that Gasem had bought from the grocer, and they showed it to the missionary. "How interesting!" exclaimed Mr. Donaldson. "If you would like to have a whole copy, I will give you one." And, putting a nicely bound New Testament in the hands of Muhammad, he said, "Accept this as a gift, and read it carefully. It will tell you all about Jesus Christ and how you can be saved from your sins by believing in him."

"Oh, thank you!" said the brothers. "And if there are things we can't understand, could we ask you to explain the book to us?"

Mr. Donaldson readily agreed, and after that the two men came to him every week for a Bible lesson. They were Muslims, but from studying the Word of God they learned that Jesus is the only

Savior, and they decided to trust in him and follow him. After months of study, they were baptized and became Christians, and later also their families were baptized.

Thus God used the wrapping paper about the cheese—a page from his Word—to lead Gasem and Muhammad and their families to Christ, the Bread of Life.

BIBLE READING: MATTHEW 7:7–11

4

They Broke My Leg and They Broke My Head

It was a beautiful afternoon, and the sick men in the Christian hospital in Meshed were enjoying the sunshine as they lay in their beds on the upstairs porch. How thankful they were for this hospital, where the missionary doctors and nurses cared for them so kindly and so skillfully!

Once there had been no good hospital in Meshed to which poor sick men and women and children could go for healing. But, as I told you in a previous story, a young doctor in America named Rolla Hoffman heard of the need of many people in Iran for medical care, and he decided he would go to help them. He remembered that Jesus had said to his disciples, "Go and heal the sick." Dr. Hoffman loved Jesus and wanted to obey him. So after a long journey by ship and by horse-drawn wagons, he came to Meshed in 1916 and joined Mr. Esselstyn.

What a time Dr. Hoffman had setting up a hospital! He rented a building, hired a carpenter to make beds and tables and chairs, and employed some men and women to help him care for the sick people who soon began to come to him with their pains and diseases. He was able, with God's blessing, to help many of them get well and go home again. When they told their friends about the good doctor in Meshed, other sick people came to him. So many came that he had no room for them in his little hospital. What could he do? He wrote to his friends in America to tell them of the need for a bigger and better hospital building in Meshed.

When Christians in America heard of this need, they said, "Surely we must give Dr. Hoffman a good building in which to care for the sick people and to show Christ's love to them. Suppose we ask the children in the Sunday schools of all the Presbyterian churches to do this." Everybody thought this was a fine idea. So in many churches the story of Dr. Hoffman's work was told, and the boys and girls and grown-ups in the Sunday schools were offered the opportunity to give money to build the Meshed hospital. Did they do it? Indeed they did! So many pennies and nickels and dimes and dollars were given in a special Easter offering that a nice big building was put up in Meshed in 1924 by the Iranian masons and carpenters and tinsmiths. How happy the doctors and nurses were to have this good place in which to serve Christ and help the sick! In addition to the rooms, a big upstairs porch was built where beds could be placed in nice weather and where the patients could enjoy the sunshine and see the trees and flowers in the yard. Before the new hospital was built, Dr. Hartman Lichtwardt came to work with Dr. Hoffman. So the two doctors were able to care for many sick people.

As I was saying, on a beautiful afternoon some years after the building of the new hospital, a number of sick men were lying in their beds on the porch in the sunshine. I climbed the stairs and went out onto the porch to visit them and to cheer them and to pray for them. I went from bed to bed, speaking a friendly word to each patient, for most of them were lonely and tired. At last I came to a bed on which lay an old man with a white beard. "*Salaam!* [peace to you!]" I said. "How are you feeling, old man?"

"Thank God, I am much better," he said.

"Why are you here?" I asked. "What is the matter with you?"

"They broke my head," he replied.

"Broke your head!" I exclaimed. "Who broke your head?"

"Yes," he went on, "they broke my head, and they also broke my leg. I was out in the desert alone, and they attacked me."

I looked at the old man, and I said to him, "Tell me, are you a shepherd?"

"Yes," he replied. "I am a shepherd. One night I was out in the desert with my sheep. Suddenly I saw three men coming toward me, and I knew they were robbers who wanted to steal my sheep. I was afraid, for they were three and I was only one. So I turned and ran toward the village. As I was running, I thought about my sheep and looked back to see what was happening to them. What do you think they were doing? They were all running after me! I said to myself, 'These poor sheep expect me to protect them; I can't leave them and run away!'

So I turned back and fought the robbers. They had a shovel, and with that they hit me on the leg and broke my leg, and they also hit me on the head and broke my head. And I fell down on the ground unconscious."

"What happened to the sheep?" I asked.

"Oh," he replied, "while I was fighting the robbers, all the sheep got to the village. Not one of them was lost."

"And what then happened to you?" I asked.

"In the morning," he replied, "someone found me and picked me up and brought me here to this hospital. The doctor has been kind to me, and God has been gracious. I am getting well."

"You are a true shepherd," I said to the old man. "You loved your sheep more than you loved your own life, and you risked your life to save your sheep. Now I want to tell you about another shepherd who loved his flock so much that he really did die for them."

I opened the Persian New Testament that I had in my hand and read from John 10 what Jesus said: "I am the good shepherd. The good shepherd lays down his life for the sheep. He who is a hireling and not a shepherd, whose own the sheep are not, sees the wolf coming and leaves the sheep and flees; and the wolf snatches them and scatters them. He flees because he is a hireling and cares nothing for the sheep. I am the good shepherd. . . . And I lay down my life for the sheep."

Then I told the old shepherd how Jesus Christ had come from heaven to save us and how he died on the cross to give us life. The old man did not know how to read, and he had never before heard about Jesus, the Good Shepherd. When his head and his leg healed and he went back to his flock of sheep,

I hope that he remembered that Jesus is his shepherd, and it was really Jesus Christ who had sent the good doctors and nurses to Meshed to care for him and for thousands of others who were sick and injured.

I hope you have learned by heart a psalm of David which I learned when I was a little boy and which I have loved all my life. It begins, "The Lord is my shepherd, I shall not want." If you can't repeat it perfectly, please memorize it now.

BIBLE READING: PSALM 23

5

SOWING AND REAPING IN SEISTAN

In the winter of the year 1921, if you had been standing near the road that goes from Meshed toward the south, you would have seen an interesting sight. Five covered wagons, like the prairie schooners you have seen in pictures, each drawn by four spirited horses, were moving down the road, one after another. The wagons were loaded with trunks and boxes and bedding, and in three of the wagons were seated some American missionaries. I was in one of them. In one of the wagons a baby girl, snugly wrapped in warm blankets, lay near her parents in her little tin bathtub, which took the place of a cradle. Where were these missionaries going? They were on a six-hundred-mile journey from Meshed to Seistan. The Russian armies were threatening to invade Iran, and it was decided that some of the missionaries should leave Meshed and go south to

Seistan to work there for a time. There were no cars in Meshed, so we had to travel in wagons, just as the pioneers did in America in 1849, when they went west for gold.

The journey was a difficult one. The horses could pull the wagons only twenty or twenty-five miles a day. The dirt road was rough, and much of the country we passed through was barren, with no inhabitants. On the way, the two doctors became quite ill, and we had to stay in a little village for two weeks till they were well enough to travel. Finally, after six weeks on the road, we reached the region of Seistan and stopped in the little town of Zabul. Perhaps the baby enjoyed the journey more than anyone else.

If you look at the map of Iran, you will see that Seistan is located near the point where Iran and Afghanistan and Pakistan meet. Long ago it was a fertile region watered by the Helmund River, which flows down from the high mountains of Afghanistan. In this region were some large and important towns. But as a result of wars and bad government, Seistan had become a desert region. The water of the Helmund was not used to irrigate the land, so crops would not grow, and there were few trees to be seen. Every year in the springtime a strong wind blew almost without stopping. It was called the "one-hundred-and-twenty-day wind." It came always from the same direction, bringing clouds of dust and dirt from the dry deserts. As they walked about, people wore handkerchiefs over their faces to keep the dirt out of their eyes and mouths.

Most of the people who lived in Seistan in 1921 were very poor. They did not have good food to eat or good homes to live in. Many of them were weak and sick, and there were no good doctors to care for them. Most of the children did not learn to read and write, for there were few schools. It seemed that there was almost nobody to help these needy people. So the missionaries from Meshed cleaned up a dirty old building and turned it into a hospital, and there they began to treat the crowds of sick people who came to them every day. No doubt the people of Zabul were thankful that at last doctors had come to help them.

The doctors showed the love of Christ to the people by the way they cared for them and helped to make them well. I wanted to tell the people who Jesus was and how he had healed the sick when he was on earth. I wanted them to know how loving and kind he was to the poor people who came to him. I used to read stories from the Bible in the Persian language to the people who were waiting to see the doctor, and I hoped and prayed that some of them would believe in Jesus and follow him. But as far as I knew, no one did. It was discouraging. The doctors were happy when their patients got well, but it seemed to me that I had not been able to help anyone find new life and hope and joy through faith in Christ. After several months, the doctors and their wives and the baby girl went back to Meshed, for the Russians did not come into Iran. Later I, too, left Seistan and, riding half the way on horseback and the other half in a wagon, returned to Meshed.

Some years passed. Then an Iranian Christian, who when he was baptized took the name Hopeful, went from Meshed to Seistan to sell Bibles to the people. When he returned, he joyfully told me the good news that he had found a Christian in Seistan, whose name was Sardar Nazar Khan (*sardar* means chief). He said this man was an important person, for he was a chieftain among the people on the Afghan border. He was not

ashamed or afraid to tell people that he was a Christian, for he
had invited other chiefs to his house and encouraged them to
read the Bible. When I heard this news I was happy, and I hoped
that some day I might return to Seistan and meet this Christian brother. I wondered how this man had heard of Christ and
had decided to follow him.

Twenty years after my first visit to Seistan, it became possible for me to go to that region once more. This time I went
with Hopeful, and we traveled not in a covered wagon but in
the front seat of a truck. We went not to Zabul, which is some
distance off the main road, but to Zahedan, where the railroad
line from India ended. "How I wish we could go to Zabul on
our return journey to Meshed," I said to Hopeful as we rode
along. "I *do* want to see that Christian man you told me about!"

"I, too, hope we will see him," replied Hopeful. "Perhaps he
will come to Zahedan. If he knew you were there, I am sure
he would come. He told me he wanted very much to see you."

We spent several days in Zahedan, selling Christian books
to people in the bazaar and meeting with a few other Christians in the home of Dr. and Mrs. Satralker, missionaries who
had come from India and who had a small Christian hospital
in Zahedan. One day I called on the governor, and he told me
the terrible news he had just heard on the radio: the Japanese
had attacked the American fleet at Pearl Harbor.

Finally the time came for us to return to Meshed, but we
had seen and heard nothing of the *sardar*. Then, the day before
we left, Hopeful came from the bazaar with a beaming face
and good news. "The *sardar* is here!" he exclaimed. "I have seen
him. He is the guest of the governor. He will come to see you

at three o'clock this afternoon." How happy and how excited I was as I waited for his arrival!

Promptly at three o'clock there was a knock at the gate of the Satralker home, and when the door was opened the *sardar* entered. I had imagined he would be a big man wearing baggy white pantaloons, such as the tribesmen on the border wear, with a full black beard and a turban wrapped around his head. How surprised was I to see a clean-shaven man dressed as though he had just come from London or New York! I greeted him warmly, saying, *"Salaam!"* and invited him to be seated. Then I said, "Excuse my curiosity, but I have heard that you are a Christian. Is that true?"

"Yes," replied the *sardar.* "I have been a Christian a long time. I was baptized thirteen years ago."

"I am so glad to know that," I said. "When did you first believe in Christ?" I knew that he, like all the people of that region, must have been a Muslim.

"That was twenty years ago," he replied.

I wondered how he had heard of Christ and had been influenced to change his religion and become a Christian, for it is often a difficult and sometimes dangerous thing for a Muslim to do. So I said, "Who was it that told you about Jesus Christ?"

"No one told me," replied the *sardar.*

"Well," I said, "if no one told you about Christ, how did you know him and believe in him?"

"I learned about him from reading the Bible," said our brother.

Now I was more puzzled than ever, so I asked him where he had gotten a Bible, for at that time there was no one in that part of Iran who had Bibles to sell.

The *sardar* smiled at me and said, "I got it from you—but didn't you then have a beard?"

"You got it from me!" I exclaimed. "Yes, I was in Zabul twenty years ago, and then I had a beard. But I don't remember meeting you or selling you a Bible."

"Yes, you did," he replied. "I was a young man and lived in a village. I came to Zabul where you were, and I visited you. I asked for a big Persian Bible, and you gave it to me. We had no conversation, except that you told me that this book was the Word of God and that I should take good care of it. I took it to my home and read it carefully. Through it I became acquainted with Jesus Christ. I believed in him and became a Christian. After seven years, an English missionary came here, and he baptized me in my home. I made a big cross and hung it on the wall to let my friends know I had become a Christian. Once, when the other *sardars* wanted to rebel and fight against the king of Iran, I refused to join them. I told them that my new religion taught peace and not warfare, and I persuaded them not to go to war."

"Have you ever taken the Communion, eaten the bread and drunk from the cup, as Christ told his disciples to do in memory of him?" I asked.

"Yes, just once, at my baptism," he replied.

"If you would like to take it again," I said, "come to my room early tomorrow morning, before I leave for Meshed. We will have the Communion together."

So early next morning in the home of the Satralkers we ate the bread and drank from the cup, as Jesus commanded. It was the *sardar's* second Communion, and how happy he and all of us were! Then Hopeful and I got into the truck and started on our seven-hundred-mile journey to Meshed. As we rode along, we praised God that he had made it possible for us to see our brother in Christ, the *sardar*. And I remembered a verse in the Bible that says, "Let us not grow weary in well-doing, for in due season we shall reap, if we do not lose heart" (Gal. 6:9). The work in Seistan, which had seemed so discouraging, had not been for nothing, for at least one man had been saved by faith in Jesus Christ.

BIBLE READING: ACTS 8:26–39

6

Everything You Need for the Journey

When you go on a journey, what do you take with you? Surely you will take some books to read or some toys to play with while you are in the bus or on the plane. And, of course, you will take in your suitcase the clothes you will need while you are away from home. But would you take a bottle of water or a bag of lunch? Probably not, for food and drink would be given you on the plane, and if you were traveling by bus, you could easily buy what you wanted at one of the rest stops along the way.

But if you had been going on a journey in Iran fifty years ago through places where there were no planes or trains or buses, as there are now, you would have ridden in a carriage or a wagon or on the back of a horse or a donkey. And you would then have taken with you bread to satisfy your hunger and water to quench your thirst along the way. For you might have traveled over barren country where no one lived and where no food or drink could be found.

As I told you in the previous story, I once spent about nine months in Zabul in the region of Seistan, in the eastern part of Iran. You can find it on the map. Zabul is about twenty-five miles from the border of Afghanistan, a country into which at that time Christian missionaries were not permitted to enter. I knew I could not go into this land, but I thought I might at least go to the border and look across into Afghanistan. For it was my hope that I might one day enter and tell the people about Jesus Christ. So I decided that before returning to Meshed, I would go as close as I could to this closed land.

There was no regular road from Zabul to the border, only a path for camels and donkeys, and no one lived in this desolate region. So I told my servant, Hasan, to hire two donkeys, one for him and one for me. We got ready some good whole-wheat bread and some cheese and raisins for our lunch, and we filled a *kuze* (an earthen jug that keeps water cool) with water. Then early the next morning we started off eastward, riding on our donkeys toward the border of Afghanistan. All day we rode along the narrow path with low bushes on either side, and not one person did we see along the way. It was after dark when we arrived at a little village, and there we spent the night in an empty room that a kind person let us use. But we didn't sleep very well, for a wedding celebration was going on and there was lots of noise in the village.

Before daylight the next morning, we got up and ate some bread and cheese and went on toward the border. Soon we came to a river. We knew this was the Helmund, a stream that comes down from the melting snows way off in the high mountains of Afghanistan and waters the region of Seistan. Here the river formed the border between Iran and Afghanistan. I got off the donkey, stood near the bank of the river, and looked across to the other side. It was a dry and barren land, and not a house or a living soul was to be seen anywhere. So I put on my swimsuit, which I had brought along, and gave my camera to Hasan, and I swam to the other side and stood on the soil of Afghanistan while Hasan took my picture. There was nothing I could carry back with me as a keepsake of my brief visit to the closed land except some dry grass. So I gathered a handful and took it with me; I still have a few pieces of it among my treasures. This was my one and only journey into Afghanistan.

I hastened back across the river and changed my clothes. Then we mounted our donkeys and started on our way to Zabul. In the afternoon the sun was hot, and we were tired from our long journey. We were dozing as we rode slowly on our donkeys along the path, I in front and Hasan behind. Suddenly a man came out of the bushes just in front of me and began to walk on ahead of me. I like to be friendly with people I meet, so I called out to him "*Salaam!*" According to the custom, he should have said *"Salaam"* to me in reply, but he did not. Instead, he pulled his cloak over his head and walked on in silence. From that I knew that he did not feel friendly to me. He knew from seeing my foreign clothes and my big sun helmet that I was not a follower of his prophet Muhammad, so he thought I was his enemy. Sometimes the people on the border kill those who do not accept their Muslim religion, so I was not happy about the way this man was acting.

All at once the man turned about and shouted back at me, "Why don't you accept our prophet?" What he meant was: Why have you not believed in Muhammad? Of course, I didn't want to get into an argument with this Muslim and make him angry, but I did want to tell him the truth. So I prayed that God would tell me what to say. Then I politely called to him and said, "Sir, if you give me permission I will tell you."

"Speak!" he said.

So as I rode along on the donkey while he walked some distance ahead of me, I said to him something like this: "My friend, you and I are travelers, passing through this desolate country, and we hope to reach our homes safely this evening. We well know that if a traveler is to reach his home, at least four things are necessary: a road, light, bread, and water. Without this path we are following, we would lose our way and never reach our homes. But even when there is a road we need light. When night comes and there is no light from the sun or the moon, we could easily get off the road and get lost in the jungle and perish. We also need bread to give us strength, and both you and I have with us food that we can eat when we get hungry. Then with new strength we will go on our way. And, finally, we need water. Since there are no springs or streams of water along our road, we have brought with us sufficient water to quench our thirst and refresh us. So we have these four things necessary for our journey, a road, light, bread, and water, and with God's help we will reach our homes tonight.

"Now," I continued, "what I have been saying is a parable, and it has a spiritual meaning. For we are both on another journey—the journey of life. We came into this world; we are now passing through it; and we hope when we die to go to our true and everlasting home in heaven. If we wish to make this spiritual journey safely and happily, we need those same four things I spoke of: a road, light, bread, and water. You think I am a Christian, do you not? Yes, I am a Christian, and I believe in Jesus Christ. You Muslims consider him a great prophet, and you know he always spoke the truth.

"Let me tell you some of the things Jesus said. He once said, 'I am the way; no one comes to the Father, but by me' [John 14:6]. Jesus claimed to be the one true way to God. Since I have faith in him, I have a road, which I have been following since I was a child. It is a very good road, and it leads straight to God and to the heavenly home. So I am not lost; I am on the right road, and I am sure if I follow it I will reach home at last.

"Jesus also said, 'I am the light of the world; he who follows me will not walk in darkness but will have the light of life' [John 8:12]. Jesus is my light, and he always makes my way bright. I will not stumble and fall in the darkness or lose the way, for I can see where I am going. His light shines in my heart and makes me happy as I travel along. So, you see, I have both a road and light for my journey.

"I spoke also about the need for bread. Jesus once said, 'I am the bread of life; he who comes to me shall not hunger' [John 6:35]. When we eat wheat bread, it satisfies our bodies for a few hours, and then we get hungry again. But Jesus satisfies the hunger of our hearts. He is himself heavenly bread. And when we take him into our minds and hearts, he gives us new life and strength, and we are able to go on our journey to the very end. I have been feeding on this true bread all my life. It is very good and gives strength to my spirit. I know I will not get tired and fall down but will be able to reach my heavenly home.

"The fourth thing that is needed for the journey is water to refresh the traveler when he gets thirsty. And Jesus gives not only bread but also water. He said, 'If anyone thirst, let him come to me and drink. . . . Whoever drinks of the water that I shall give him will never thirst again' (John 7:37; 4:14). This promise also is true, for I have drunk this water of life, and it has quenched my spiritual thirst. When I have been sad or discouraged, the water that Jesus gives has refreshed me and made me glad.

"So you see, my friend, that I have in Jesus Christ everything that I need for the journey of life: a road, light, bread, and water. What else do I need? Why should I believe in anyone else?" I meant: What need do I have of your prophet Muhammad?

When the man heard this, he replied in a friendly tone, "You have spoken the truth." Seeing that he no longer thought me his enemy, I got off my donkey, told Hasan to bring it along behind, and went forward and joined my fellow traveler. For several hours we walked together along the path through the bushes. Since he was now willing to listen, I told him the wonderful story of the life of Jesus Christ—that he was born of Mary, became a great teacher of God's truth, healed the sick, and loved the people of all the world so much that he gave his life to save them from their sins. I told him that he came to life again on the third day after his crucifixion and that after forty days he went to heaven, where he is today. I told the man that Jesus is with all who believe in him at all times and that he will one day come again to raise the dead to life and to be the judge of all the people of the world.

The man listened with great interest. Finally he stopped and said to me, "I live just over here. Come and spend the night with me."

"Thank you very much," I replied, "you are most kind. But it is getting late, and I must hasten on to Zabul tonight. Please excuse me and let me go on my way."

He gave his consent, and I said a prayer for him. He then went off into the bushes toward his home, and I got on my donkey and traveled along with Hasan till we reached Zabul in safety. I never saw my fellow traveler again. But I hope he followed the Way and walked in the Light and ate the Bread and drank the Water of Life of which I told him. If he did so, he will surely reach the heavenly home at last. And so will you and I if we trust in Christ.

BIBLE READING: JOHN 4:5—15

7

THE SHEPHERD BOY
WHO LOST HIS SHEEP

id you ever see a town with a wall all around it? I am
sure the town in which you live has no wall about
it. But once I was in a big town in Iran named Sabzevar that was surrounded by a high wall. The wall was to keep
out enemies or robbers or wild animals that might want to
come in and hurt the people. So if you wanted to go into Sabzevar, you had to enter through one of the gates. The gates were
very big—big enough for horses or wagons or camels to go
through. At night the heavy wooden doors of the gates were
shut and locked, and no one could go in or out unless he woke
up the gatekeeper and asked him to open the door.

Why did I go to Sabzevar? I went there to tell the people
about Jesus Christ. Most of the people in that town did not
know how much Jesus loves us and how he came to this world

to save us from sin and make us good like him. They were not Christians; they were Muslims. They thought their prophet Muhammad was better than Jesus, so they followed what he said. As you know, Jesus Christ loves all the people in the world and wants everybody to know and love and obey him. So I went to Sabzevar, taking with me a supply of the books that tell about Jesus, such as the gospel of Matthew and the gospel of John. The people there did not know English, so these books were in their language, which was Persian.

In Iran every town has a shopping center, which is called a bazaar. There the shopkeepers sell the things the people need, such as sugar, tea, cheese, rice, bread, cloth, shoes, carpets for the floor, and many other things. Each day I would go to the bazaar in Sabzevar with my books, looking for men who might want to read them. At that time no women ever worked in the bazaars of Iran. So I would go to a shop and say to the shopkeeper, "I have here a book about Jesus Christ; would you like to have it?" He might reply, "I am sorry, but I cannot read, so I do not need the book." There were many people in Iran at that time who never had the opportunity to go to school and learn to read and write. Another man might say, "I cannot read, but my son goes to school; he will read the book for me." He would give me two rials, and I would put in his hand one of the books. But sometimes a man would say, "No, I follow Muhammad, and I have his book, the Koran; so I do not want your book about Jesus." Whenever I heard that reply, I felt sad, and I would go on to another shop. I always prayed that some of the men would read the books and would want to come to see me in my room in the evening to learn more about Christ. A few did come, and several believed in him and became Christians.

One afternoon I decided to take a walk. The streets in Sabzevar were narrow, and it was no fun to walk in them. So I went to one of the gates in order to go outside and walk in the open country. Just as I was about to go out the gate I had to stop, for something was coming in. What do you think it was? It wasn't a donkey, and it wasn't a camel—it was a sheep! I am sure you have seen a sheep, haven't you—either out in a field or perhaps in the zoo? But I think you never saw a sheep like this one. The sheep you saw had a funny little thing attached to its rear end that we call a tail. But this sheep had a *real* tail! It was like a pillow, and the more grass the sheep ate, the bigger his tail became. While I waited at the gate, another fat-tailed sheep came in, and then many followed—a whole flock of sheep entered Sabzevar!

You have seen a sheep, but after the sheep came something I think you have never seen. After the sheep came a shepherd! Do you know what that is? Well, a shepherd is a person who takes care of the sheep; he is the baby sitter for the sheep! The sheep that you saw grazing in a field didn't need anyone to take care of them, for there was a fence around the field to keep them in and grass and water for them to eat and drink. And there were no wolves or robbers to hurt the sheep, so they had no need for a shepherd.

But in some countries, like Iran, you never see sheep without a shepherd. Usually the sheep are not kept in fenced fields but are taken out to the plains or the mountains to feed, and they always have shepherds with them to guide them and to guard them from robbers and wild animals. Sometimes the shepherds are old men with long white beards, and sometimes they are boys. I have seen boys and girls taking care of a flock

THE SHEPHERD BOY WHO LOST HIS SHEEP

of pretty little lambs. Often the shepherds have big, fierce dogs to help them drive away the wolves that might want to kill and eat the sheep.

The shepherd who followed the sheep through the gate into Sabzevar was not an old man; he was a boy about twelve years of age. When he passed me I said to him, *"Salaam!"* The shepherd boy answered, *"Salaam."* Then I said to him, "Do all these sheep belong to you?"

"No," he replied, "they belong to the owner; I am their shepherd."

"Well, Mr. Shepherd," I said, "where did you take your flock of sheep today?"

"I took them to the mountain for grass and water," he replied, "and now I am taking them home for the night."

While we were talking, the sheep went ahead along the narrow street toward their home. "Your sheep have left you," I said, "you had better run after them." Then I said to the shepherd *"Khoda Hafiz!* [God be your keeper, or good-bye.]"

He replied, *"Khoda Hafiz!"* and away he ran to catch up with the sheep.

I went through the gate into the fields outside the town and followed a path that led toward the mountain. The air was clear and cool, and I had a fine walk, looking up at the blue sky and away to the beautiful mountains in the distance. When I noticed that the sun was about to set, I thought I had better turn around and go back to Sabzevar. As I did so, I saw someone running toward me from the town. When he drew near, I saw it was the shepherd boy. *"Salaam!"* I said. "Where are you going? Why are you running so fast?"

"*Salaam!*" he replied as he panted for breath. "When I got home and counted the sheep, one of them was missing. I have to find it!"

"I hope you will find it soon," I said, "for night is coming fast." We said *"Khoda Hafiz"* to each other, and he ran off toward the mountain while I returned to the town.

Several days later, as I was walking along one of the narrow streets of Sabzevar, I met the shepherd boy coming toward me. *"Salaam!"* I said. "Did you find the sheep you lost?"

"Yes," he replied with a big smile. "I found it and brought it home!" And wasn't he happy that he found the lost sheep!

"Good for you," I said. "You arc a real shepherd!"

And I remembered a lovely story that Jesus once told about a shepherd who had a big flock of a hundred sheep and lost one of them. What did he do? He didn't say, "I have ninety-nine

sheep, and I don't need that one that got lost." No, he left the ninety-nine sheep and went after the one lost sheep. At last he found it, and he was happy that a wolf had not eaten it up. He put it on his shoulders and carried it all the way home, and it was a heavy load. When he reached home, he called his friends to come and to be happy and to celebrate with him. "Rejoice with me," he said, "for I have found my sheep that was lost!"

This story is called a parable because it has a special meaning. Who do you think is meant by the kind shepherd? The shepherd is surely Jesus, who once said, "I am the good shepherd." And who is meant by the lost sheep? We are the lost sheep, for anyone who does not know the way home is lost. We people in this world did not know the way to God; so we were lost. But Jesus came from heaven to find us and to bring us safely home to God. If he had not come for us, we would have perished, like the sheep in the mountains. I am sure that that sheep wanted to say, "Thank you!" to the shepherd who saved it. Since it could not talk, perhaps it licked the hand of the kind shepherd. And we love Jesus, our Good Shepherd, because he loved us so much that he even gave his life to save us and to bring us back to God.

Yes, Jesus is our Great Shepherd. And what is a missionary? A missionary is a little shepherd who goes to find the sheep and the lambs that are lost—the people who do not know God—to tell them about Jesus and to help them to come to him to be saved.

BIBLE READINGS: LUKE 15:3—7; JOHN 10:7—15

8

HOW THE BIBLE SPEAKS IN THE PERSIAN LANGUAGE

In several of the stories I have told you, I said that the Bibles or portions of the Bible that we gave to people in Iran were in the Persian language. Of course, the Bible was not written in Persian or in English. Most of the Old Testament writers wrote their books in Hebrew, and the New Testament was written in Greek. We are able to read the Bible in English because men who knew Hebrew and Greek translated it into our language; that is, they put the message of God into language that we can understand. In the same way, that message was put into the beautiful Persian language, which most of the people of Iran understand. Who did this great work? Let me tell you!

In the year 1811 there came to the city of Shiraz in the southern part of Iran a man named Henry Martyn. Though he was only thirty years of age, Martyn had become a great scholar. He had gone from his native land, which was England, to India in the year 1807 to serve Christ, and there he had learned three languages in order to translate the Bible into each of them. One of these languages was Persian. Since the place where the best Persian was spoken was Shiraz, Martyn went there from India to make his translation as good as possible. His health was not good, and the long journey on horseback in the great heat from Bushire, where he got off the ship, to Shiraz was difficult for him. In Shiraz he began to feel better, and for nearly a year he worked hard with a Persian scholar to put God's message into the language of Iran.

When Henry Martyn finished translating the New Testament, he started off again on horseback to Teheran, the capital—a journey of six hundred miles—hoping that he would be able to present a copy of the Holy Book to the *Shah* (the king of Iran). But he was disappointed, for the Shah was not willing to receive him. So he traveled west to Tabriz, another long journey on horseback. The sun was hot, and Martyn was sick when he arrived in Tabriz. (You can follow his journey across Iran on your map.) Some kind English people in Tabriz cared for him till he got better. Then he started to go to England, but the journey across Turkey on horseback was too hard for him, and he died on the way in 1812.

What happened to his translation of the New Testament? Was it lost? No, it was not. The British ambassador presented one copy to the Shah in Teheran, who expressed appreciation and ordered that it be read to him. Another copy was taken to Russia by this same ambassador, and it was published there in 1815. This was the first time that the whole New Testament in the Persian language was put in a book that people could buy and read. A copy of this first edition was kept in a special place in the church in Shiraz, and there is another copy in the church in Tabriz. I have seen both of these precious volumes. Some years later, a man named William Glen translated the Old Testament into Persian. Then people in Iran had all of God's Word in their own language.

But how were people to get these books? There were some Christians in England who had formed the Bible Society, the purpose of which was to print the Bible in as many languages as possible, so that all the people of the world could learn about God and about the Savior Jesus Christ. Many thousands of copies of the Bible, or parts of the Bible, were printed in Persian and other languages with money given by people who loved Christ and wanted others to know him. Some of these books were sent to Iran, and a man was appointed to be in charge of the distribution of the books to people who wanted them. This man chose a few Iranian Christians to work for the Bible Society.

These men, known as booksellers, went all over the country, selling the precious books. But they really did not sell them. They knew that people would be more eager to keep the books and to read them carefully if they paid something for them, so the booksellers took some money from those who wanted the books. But they took very little, so that even poor people could have the Word of God. For example, the gospel of Luke, which was worth twenty-five cents, might have been given for five cents, and a Bible worth five dollars was sold for one dollar. For many years, these faithful booksellers went to thousands of towns and villages in all parts of Iran, and as a result millions of people—Christians, Jews, and Muslims—have been given the opportunity to read God's message in their own language. I want to tell you about one of these brave and faithful men who distributed the Bible in Iran.

Baron Nicola is an Armenian, and in the Armenian language "Baron" is used for "Mr." The Armenian people have been Christians for more than sixteen hundred years. Many years ago some of them came from their country to Iran. They are citizens of Iran, but they usually speak both Armenian and Persian. Many of the booksellers of the Bible Society were Armenians. When Baron Nicola was a young man, he and his wife jumped onto the back of a horse and dashed away from their home in Rezaieh in the western part of Iran to save their lives from cruel enemies, who were trying to kill the Christians.

In their flight they came to Hamadan, and there Baron Nicola got a job as a nurse in the American Christian hospital. Not only did he help the doctor take care of the sick men, but he also read the Bible to them and told them about Christ. He loved this Bible work so much that after a time he decided to become a bookseller of the Bible Society. So for many years Baron Nicola traveled all over Iran—sometimes by wagon, sometimes by horse or donkey, and later by truck or bus— taking the Word of God to people who had neither heard it nor seen a Bible. Not all the people welcomed him, for some of the Muslims did not want people to read the Bible and believe in Christ. Several times evil men tried to kill the brave servant of Christ, but God protected him. When I was living in Meshed, Baron Nicola and his family came there to distribute Bibles, and we often traveled and worked together.

Once Baron Nicola, two other Christian men, and I went to the town of Kuchan, about one hundred miles north of Meshed, to sell Christian books and to talk to interested people about Jesus Christ. We stayed there several days, and just before Christmas we started back to Meshed, so that we could be with our families on that happy day. At that time there were no buses in Iran, but there were a few trucks that carried goods and passengers from one city to another. We found a truck in Kuchan that was to go to Meshed, so we decided to travel in it. The truck had a top over it, and on the two sides was a wire screening, and the back was open. A lot of other people were going in the same truck. We all put our bedding and baggage on the floor and sat on it with our legs crossed, packed together like sardines in a can.

The ground was covered with snow, and it was cold. The wind blew through the open sides of the truck. We pulled our coats over our heads to keep warm. We hoped to be in Meshed for supper—but we were not!

We had been bumping along the rough road for perhaps an hour when suddenly our driver put on the brakes and turned the truck sharply off the road to the right. We rose up, wondering what on earth had happened. A moment later the driver released the brakes, turned around, and started back toward Kuchan. When we looked out the open back end of the truck, we saw the reason for this change of direction: in the road where we had turned around stood two men with guns in their hands. They were bandits, and they wanted to rob us. When they saw our truck was going away from them, they began shooting at us. Several bullets came into the truck, and one of them slightly wounded one of the passengers near us.

Baron Nicola was sitting close to me. When he saw the robbers shooting at us, what do you think he did? He threw himself on top of me, so that the bullets would hit him and not hit me! Wasn't that a wonderful thing for him to do? He was ready to give his life for his friend. Fortunately, he was not hit, and neither was I. No one in the truck was seriously wounded. We returned to Kuchan in safety. When we next started for Meshed, some soldiers came along in the truck to guard us. What happened to the bandits I do not know, but I heard that they had been caught and punished. We arrived home in time for Christmas, thankful to God for taking care of us.

Ever since then, I have loved and honored Baron Nicola, not only for the great work he has done for Christ in Iran, but also because he risked his life for me. I remember how Jesus said, "Greater love has no man than this, that a man lay down his life for his friends." That was what Jesus did for us; he loved us so much that he died for us. And because he loved us, we love him and want to serve him. As we sing in the lovely hymn:

> O, dearly, dearly has he loved,
> And we must love him, too,
> And trust in his redeeming blood,
> And try his works to do.

BIBLE READING: JOHN 15:12—14

9

WHY THE WOLF CAN'T
ENTER THE FOLD

Before the coming of cars and buses to Iran, the Christians who wanted to take the good news of Jesus Christ to the millions of people who lived in the towns and villages usually rode on donkeys or walked. Of course, a donkey can't travel as fast as a car, and instead of taking an hour in a car to go from one town to another, it would take a day or two to make the journey by donkey. I liked to ride along slowly on a donkey, and sometimes I got off the donkey and walked. It was good exercise to ride or to walk twenty miles a day. Also, there were often other people riding and walking along the road. Since no cars ever came to push the travelers off the road, it was often possible to talk with them about Jesus Christ without any interruption.

On one of these missionary journeys, I met a boy riding on a donkey, and, since we were going in the same direction, I was able to tell him about Jesus Christ. When I saw he was inter-ested, I said to him, "I have a little book in my pocket that tells me more about Jesus. Would you like to have it?"

"Yes," he replied, "I go to school, and I know how to read; please let me have the book."

I took from my pocket the gospel of Matthew in Persian, and I handed it to him. He looked at it, read a little, and said, "I want this book. May I keep I?"

"Yes," I replied, "but there is a price you must pay. Will you please give me one rial?"

The boy looked disappointed and said, "I don't have any money."

"Well, what do you have that you could give for the book?" I asked.

"I have some barley bread," he said. "Would you take that?"

Barley bread is not as good as wheat bread, and usually only the very poor people eat it. But I said, "Of course I will take it. Give me a piece of your bread."

So he broke off a piece and gave it to me. Then he went on his way, reading the book as he rode on his donkey. He had exchanged barley bread for the bread of life, and both he and I were happy.

On another journey, I caught up with a group of men and women and children who were, as I, going away from Meshed. Some were riding on donkeys, and some were walking. I said *"Salaam!"* to them, and they said *"Salaam!"* to me, and we walked along together for several miles. I learned that these people were pilgrims. They had traveled many weeks from dis-tant Isfahan to visit the tomb of the Imam Reza in Meshed, about which I told you. And now they were on their way home.

I said to one of the men, "How many times did you go to the tomb of the Imam Reza to pray while you were in Meshed?"

"We were there for two weeks," he replied, "and we visited the holy tomb every day."

"I know you made the long pilgrimage to Meshed," I said, "because you thought that if you did, God would forgive your sins and take you to heaven when you die. Has God been pleased with your pilgrimage, and has he forgiven your sins?"

"How do I know?" replied the man. "Perhaps he has, perhaps he has not; only God knows." So the pilgrims went on their weary way, not knowing whether they would be forgiven and go to heaven or not be forgiven and go to hell. How I wished that they had faith in Jesus, who died for all sinners so that all who believe in him may know that God has forgiven them and that they will surely go to heaven at last!

One afternoon in November, as several Christians and I were riding donkeys on our way to Sabzevar, a strong and cold wind began to blow in our faces. No rain had fallen for six months, and the land was so dry that the wind brought clouds of dust upon us, and we tied our handkerchiefs over our faces to keep the dirt out of our eyes and mouths. We were glad when we reached a little village by the roadside and were able to get some shelter from the stormy wind.

But in the village no room was to be found in which we could spend the night, except one in which some chickens were kept. The owner agreed to put out his chickens and let us sleep in their place! Poor chickens—I don't know where they spent the night! We soon swept the room, put up our camp cots, fixed some tea and food for our supper, and went to bed. What a wonderful sleep we had after our day of travel!

In the morning when I awoke and opened the door, what do you think I saw? A world of dazzling whiteness! The wind had brought snow, and the brown, dusty fields were hidden by a beautiful covering of the whitest thing in the world. What a sudden change had come! I thought of the prayer of David to God, when he asked that his sinful heart might be made clean: "Wash me, and I shall be whiter than snow!" (Ps. 51:7).

After we had eaten our breakfast of bread and cheese and tea, I called the man who owned the donkeys and asked him when we could start on our way to Sabzevar. "The snow is too deep for the donkeys to go through," he replied. "We will have to wait till tomorrow, when the snow will have melted and the road will be better." So we remained in the village all day.

In the morning we had a Bible lesson, and we prayed together. Then, after we had eaten some lunch, I went outside in the snow to see what I could see. There wasn't much to see but snow, snow, snow! However, a little distance from the village I saw a mound that was, like everything else, covered with snow. When I reached it, I found that earth had been piled up to make kind of a wall, and this wall was round. Inside the wall the earth had been hollowed out, so that it looked like a big bowl. Then on top of the wall of earth had been piled a lot of dry thorn bushes, the sort that grow in the desert in Iran. I walked around the circular mound till I came to an entrance. There was no door, so I walked down inside the big bowl and looked around me, wondering what this place was used for.

Just then a man came in after me. He lived in the village and, having seen me enter the enclosure, followed me to talk to me.

"*Salaam!*" I said. "Please tell me what this strange-looking place is."

"Oh," he replied, "this is the fold. This is the place to which the sheep are brought at night when the weather is warm."

"Very good," I said, "now I understand. But why were the dry thorns put on top of the mound of earth around the fold?"

"That was done," said the villager, "to keep out the wolf."

"But I don't see how those thorns could keep out a wolf," I replied. "A wolf is big and strong enough to knock down the pile of thorns, then jump into the fold and kill the sheep."

"Oh, no," responded the man. "When the wolf strikes the thorns with his paw, they make a crackling noise. That noise wakes up the shepherd, and he rushes with his big stick to the place where the wolf is and drives him away."

"But, really," I said, "the wolf doesn't need to jump over the wall. Here is the entrance, and it has no door. Why doesn't the wolf just walk in through the entrance and attack the sheep?"

"No, no," replied the man. "That is where the shepherd sleeps. He lies down in the entrance so that nobody can get into the fold. The shepherd is the door; he keeps the wolf and the robbers out of the fold of the sheep."

Next day as we were riding on our donkeys along the road, now muddy because of the melting snow, I thought much about what the villager had said to me. He said that the shepherd is the door, and that helped me understand better something Jesus said about himself. In the tenth chapter of John, Jesus first said, "I am the door." By that he meant that it is only through him that we can enter into God's fold, the place of salvation, where we are safe from the attacks of Satan, who is the wolf. Then Jesus said, "I am the good shepherd." How could he be the shepherd of the sheep if he is the door? Because the door is the shepherd, and the shepherd is the door!

Yes, we who believe in Christ are God's sheep, and you children are the lambs of the flock. The shepherd who cares for us always is Jesus Christ. Whenever we say in the twenty-third psalm, "The Lord is my shepherd, I shall not want," we know that the shepherd is Jesus, who loves us and is with us always. And whether we are awake or asleep, he is guarding us. Satan cannot touch us when we are close to him, our Good Shepherd.

BIBLE READING: JOHN 10:7—15

10

How Hasan Found the Savior

hasan was born in Meshed. When he was a little boy his father and mother used to take him with them when they visited the tomb of the Imam Reza, about which I have told you, which was near their home. Hasan liked to look up at the big golden dome over the tomb when it glittered in the sunlight. He liked to watch the crowds of people who had come on pilgrimage, some of them from foreign lands, wearing strange-looking clothes and speaking languages that the little boy could not understand. He saw how the pilgrims said the Arabic prayers at the tomb, and he learned to do it himself. Before long, he was able to go by himself to the tomb. He would take off his shoes at the door, as everybody did, and say the prayers just like the men.

The Muslim people in Iran usually don't celebrate Christmas as we do, so the boys and girls don't have Christmas trees and stockings and gifts. And they do not know that Jesus came at Christmas as God's gift to all the people of the world. But there is a day in Iran when gifts are often given to the children; that day is *Noruz,* which is the Iranian New Year. It is not January 1, like our New Year, but March 21, when spring comes to Iran. The cold winter is past, and people like to put on new clothes and to visit one another, saying *"Eid-i-shoma mobarak!"* which means, "May your holiday be happy!" It is at Noruz that parents often give new shirts or socks or shoes to their boys and new dresses and other pretty things to their girls.

One Noruz, Hasan's father gave him a beautiful pair of red leather shoes. How happy and proud he was to wear these shoes everywhere he went! Once he wore them when he was going by himself to visit the tomb of the Imam Reza. When he took them off at the door, he said to the man who kept the shoes of the pilgrims while they went inside to pray, "Be sure to take good care of my red shoes!" But when he came out, his shoes were nowhere to be seen. "Where are my shoes?" said Hasan to the shoe keeper.

"Here they are," said he as he handed Hasan a pair of old, ugly shoes.

"No, no," protested Hasan. "Those aren't my shoes! Give me my new red shoes."

The man insisted that he knew nothing of the shoes, and Hasan kept telling him to give him his shoes at once. A crowd of people gathered around to see what the quarrel was about. All at once Hasan yelled at the shoe keeper, who was seated on the floor with his robe pulled about him, "Get up!" The man rose, and underneath him were the red shoes, which he had tried to steal. Hasan grabbed them, put them on his feet, and

ran home. Never after that did he have any love for the Imam
Reza or trust in the men who served at his tomb.

When Hasan became a man, he left Iran and went north
into Turkestan, to cities that belonged to Russia. (You can find
Turkestan on the map.) Many people from Iran were living
there, so Hasan got a job working for an Iranian man who made
cakes and candies. This man was not a Muslim. He followed a
new religion called Baha'ism, and he used to talk to Hasan
about his faith. "You are not a Muslim," he said, "and you say
you are looking for the true religion. I can tell you where you
can find it. You must go to the town of Akka [Acre] on the
shore of the Mediterranean Sea. There a man named Abdul
Baha will tell you how to know God." So Hasan started for
Akka, which is a long way from Turkestan.

Hasan spent what little money he had to ride in a wagon
part of the way. Then, when his money was finished, he walked
the rest of the way. He had to have food to eat, so he made
funny little paper birds, which he sold to children for a penny
apiece. With that money he bought bread, and he would say to
his feet, "You have to carry me eight miles before I feed you!"
His faithful feet would then take him on his way, and after a
while he would sit down and eat his bread. In this way he finally
reached Akka, but his journey took him many months. How
eager he was to find the truth about God!

Was Abdul Baha able to help him find God? No, he was not.
Hasan stayed in Akka several weeks, but he finally left, deeply
disappointed. He saw that this man did not really know God,
so of course he could not help anyone else find God. When
Hasan at last returned to his native land, Iran, he had no faith
in any religion, and he did not even believe in God. He was

altogether hopeless. To lose faith in God is indeed a terrible thing.

Hasan wandered about Iran for some time, as unhappy as he could be. But God knew that he was trying to find the way to salvation and guided him back to Turkestan. There one day he saw a group of men gathered about a man who was reading from a book. Hasan had never had an opportunity to go to school, so he could not read or write. But he was smart, and he always liked to learn from other people. So he joined the group and listened carefully to what the man was reading aloud.

Who was this man? And what was the book he was reading? He was Benjamin Badal, one of the booksellers of the Bible Society. Benjamin had come all the way from Iran to Turkestan to bring God's message to the people. And God brought Hasan to him at just the right time to hear the message. The bookseller was reading the twenty-fourth chapter of the gospel of Matthew, in which Jesus told his disciples that they must beware of false christs and false prophets who were going to come and who would deceive many people and would lead them away from God.

When Hasan heard this, he said to himself, "I know who these false leaders are! They have come and have led people astray. But the one who said they were going to come is true. That was Jesus Christ, so I believe in him." He didn't know much about Jesus, but then and there he put his trust in him and decided to be a Christian.

Some time later, Hasan returned to his birthplace, Meshed. While he had been away, Christian missionaries had come there to live and work, as I told you previously, and Hasan was glad to meet them and to tell them that he was a Christian. He was bold in telling the Muslim people about his faith, and they did not like to hear what he said. So he went to Nishapur, a town about one hundred miles west of Meshed (see the map). There he rented a little room in the bazaar and invited men to come to see him and to read the Bible. Though he could not read it himself, he was able to explain the meaning to his visitors.

One man in Nishapur said he also wanted to become a Christian, and he wrote a letter to the missionaries in Meshed, asking that a minister come to Nishapur to baptize him and Hasan. So it was decided that I should go to Nishapur with one of the Christian men from Meshed. We traveled for three days by donkey, going over the high mountains between Meshed and Nishapur. We remained in Nishapur several days.

After we had explained how a person could believe in Christ and be saved and how a Christian should live, Hasan and his friend and the son of the friend were baptized. I put some water from a bowl on their heads, in the name of Jesus Christ, to show that Jesus washes away our sins and makes us clean when we believe in him. And the men promised to obey and serve Jesus Christ. Of course, there was no church in Nishapur, for the people there were Muslims, so the baptism was held in the home of Hasan's friend, where we were guests. After the baptism we had the Lord's Supper, when we ate some bread and drank some grape juice as Jesus commanded, to remember how he died for us.

You have heard of opium, I am sure. Do you know that opium is gotten from the poppy plant after the blossom has fallen off? At the time I lived in Meshed, a great deal of opium was produced in Iran, and as there were no laws against growing or using opium, many people in Iran took opium. This habit was bad for their health; it made them weak and sickly. When Hasan was baptized, he did not tell me that he had been using opium for twenty years.

One day after his baptism, he went to the place where men smoked opium. They would put a little lump of it in a pipe on a hot coal and then inhale the fumes. Hasan asked the attendant to prepare an opium pipe for him, and it was brought to him. But just as he was about to put it to his lips to smoke it, this thought came to him: *Should these lips that have taken the Lord's Supper be made unclean by taking this filthy thing?* At once he put down the pipe and walked out. It is difficult for anyone who has used opium for a long time to quit it. But Hasan stopped smoking it all at once, and he never smoked it again. He now belonged to Jesus Christ, and he did not want to do anything that was unworthy of his Savior.

If you would like to know more about Hasan, I will tell you in the next story.

Bible reading: Matthew 13:44—45

11

SANG, THE SOWER OF GOOD SEED

In the previous story I told you how Hasan searched for God and how God found him and led him to become a Christian. After his baptism, Hasan decided to take a new name, for he knew he was a new man in Christ. His friend Dr. Hoffman in Meshed suggested that he call himself Stone, which in Persian is *Sang*. You remember that was the new name that Jesus gave to his disciple Simon when he called him Peter, for in the Greek language the name Peter means stone (John 1:42). So Hasan named himself Mansur Sang, which means "victorious stone," an appropriate name for this bold soldier of Christ. From now on we will speak of Hasan as Sang.

So bold was Sang in telling people in Nishapur about Christ, and in saying that Muhammad was not a true prophet of God, that some of the Muslim people became angry and wanted to kill him. So he had to flee from the city. What was he to do next? He felt God had appointed him to be a sower of seed! You remember the parable that Jesus told about the farmer who one day went to his field to sow wheat seed. Jesus said that some of the seed fell on soil that was not good and so produced no wheat, and some of the seed fell on good ground and produced a big harvest (Matt. 13:1–23). And Jesus explained that the seed was God's Word, and the soils were the hearts and minds of people; some were good and some were bad. Before he went to heaven, Jesus commanded his disciples to go to all the people of the world and speak God's Word to them. He knew that when this heavenly seed fell on good ground, it would grow and bear fruit. That is, God's Word would be heard and believed by people who wanted to know God, and they would put their trust in Christ for salvation.

Accordingly, Sang set out for the villages in eastern Iran to sow the seed of the gospel of Christ. He often traveled on foot, for he had no money to hire a donkey. He was strong and could walk many miles a day. On his back he carried a pack, but it was not filled with clothes, for he had no clothes except what he wore. What then was in his heavy pack? It was full of seed! That is what Sang called the little books and tracts he carried with him to give to people he met, so that they could read at least a little of God's Word.

Also in his pack Sang had some medicines. There were no doctors in the villages he visited, so he took with him soda for people who had stomachaches and quinine for people who had fever. He also had an instrument for pulling teeth. Everywhere he went, people came to him with their pains and aches, and he prayed for them and gave them his medicines, and many of them got well. They would be so grateful to this kind "doctor" that they would ask him to stay in their homes for the night, and they would give him food for his next journey. And he always told the people everywhere he went about Jesus Christ.

However, when Sang said bad things about their religion, Islam, there were people who became angry and wanted to kill him. So often he would get up in the middle of the night, when everybody was asleep, and he would leave the village where he had been staying, before anyone could harm him. Once a crowd of young men decided they would pour kerosene on him and burn him up. This time he did not run away but faced the crowd alone. When the men saw his courage and the fire that flashed from his eyes, they were afraid to touch him, and they went away.

In the villages he visited there were no police. But when Sang went to the larger towns, he was often arrested by the police, who thought this strange-looking person must be a bad man. Once when he was taken before the chief of police in one of the towns, he was asked, "What are these little books you are giving to the people here?"

"These books are the Word of God, and I give them so that people will be able to know God," replied Sang.

"But," said the chief, "you give them away free of charge. That shows they are of no value; they are worthless. If they were really God's Word, as you say they are, they would have great value, and would be sold for a lot of money. We Muslims have the holy Koran, which we believe is the Word of God. It is not given away for nothing! No, if anyone wants a copy, he has to pay a big price for it."

To this Sang replied, "Sir, please let me ask you a question. What is this thing hanging on the wall of your office?"

"You stupid fellow," said the chief, "don't you know what that is? It is an electric light. Did you never see a light bulb?"

"Oh," replied Sang, pretending he had never seen an electric light before. "So that's what it is that lights your room at night. How wonderful! Please tell me, do you have to pay money for it?"

"Of course I do," replied the chief. "Every month I pay for it, and I have to pay a lot!"

"And," continued Sang, as he pointed to the open window through which the sunlight was pouring into the office of the chief, "what is this that is lighting your room right now?"

"You crazy fool," exclaimed the chief, "don't you know what that is? That is sunshine!"

"Oh," replied Sang, "how nice it is! It makes your room light and warm. I'm sure it is better than the electric light, isn't it? You must have to pay a great deal for all this light and heat."

"Of course not," said the chief, "the sunlight is free for all who want it!"

"Yes," replied Sang triumphantly, "that is it! The electric light was made by men, and so it has to be bought with money. But the sunshine is God's gift to everybody, and it is free. Your book that costs so much is a manmade book, but these books of mine

are God's Word, God's free gift to everybody. They give light and life to all who read and believe them."

Sang then gave one of his little books to each of the policemen in the room, and he gave one also to the chief, who had nothing more to say to this clever man. "Go!" said he to Sang. And Sang said a polite farewell and went on his way to another town.

After he had been traveling for several weeks, Sang liked to come back to Meshed to see his Christian friends. He loved the children of the missionaries, and they loved this jolly old fellow who played with them and sang for them and carried them on his shoulders.

Whenever he would enter the gate of our yard, the children who were playing in the yard would shout, "Mansur Sang has come! Mansur Sang has come!" and they would run to meet him. We would all give him a big welcome, let him have a bath and some clean clothes, and then give him tea and supper. He was always hungry from his long journeys, and he was able to consume large quantities of food. It seemed that he could do what a camel does: eat enough at one meal to last several days. As he drank many cups of tea, he told us thrilling stories of his wonderful adventures as he went about sowing the good seed.

Once Sang made a long journey all around Iran, during which he visited Christians in many places and sowed much gospel seed. When he was in Shiraz, where Henry Martyn had translated the New Testament into Persian, he made a journey to a village in the mountains named Qalat. There several men were glad to hear God's message and to believe in Jesus Christ. But enemies once more planned to kill the Christian messenger, and Sang had to escape in the night. It was winter, and a little stream of water that flowed from the village was partly frozen. Sang did not follow the road, where he would have been seen and caught, but went down the icy bed of the stream, getting wet and cold. In this way he was able to return to Shiraz in safety.

Later he went back to Qalat with a missionary. There he pulled many teeth, and the missionary baptized three believers. As a result of this visit, other people believed in Christ, and a beautiful little chapel was built on the hillside in which the Christians could worship God. In Qalat, Sang found some good soil in which the seed grew and bore fruit. I once visited the people in Qalat who had become Christians because of Sang's faithful work, and we had a prayer meeting in their chapel.

BIBLE READING: MATTHEW 13:3—9, 18—23

12

SA'EED, THE BRAVE AND BELOVED DOCTOR

The stories I have been telling you have been about people in the eastern part of Iran. Now I want to take you to the west, to Kurdistan. You can find it on your map. There, a hundred years ago in the town of Senna, lived a boy named Sa'eed. He belonged to the race of the Kurds, a brave and warlike people. He was a Muslim, and he had studied the Arabic Koran so much that he could understand its meaning and could also repeat much of it by heart.

Sa'eed was careful to do what his religion taught him to do. He said the prayers in Arabic, facing Mecca, five times each day. During the month of Ramadan he fasted, eating no food and drinking no water from daylight till dark. He must sometimes have gotten hungry and thirsty, but he would not eat or drink till he heard the boom of the cannon after sunset, which was the signal for the fast to end. Then during the night he would eat and drink. All the people admired this young man so much that when his father died they chose him to succeed his father as their leader when they said their prayers together in the mosque. They began to call him Mulla Sa'eed.

Then there came to Senna a man named John. He had been taught by the missionaries in Urumia (now called Rezaieh) and had a great love for Jesus Christ. He also had a great desire to tell the Muslims about Christ. John was an Assyrian and spoke their language, but he did not know the Persian language very well. So when he came to live for a time in Senna, he asked where he could find a good teacher. The people told him that young Mulla Sa'eed was the best teacher. So it was arranged that John would have Persian lessons with Sa'eed. What book do you think they used in their lessons? John wanted to use the Persian Bible, and Mulla Sa'eed agreed. So John learned Persian, and his teacher learned the truth about Jesus Christ.

Sa'eed liked his Christian teacher very much, but there were other people in Senna who did not want John to stay there. They said, "This Christian will tell us things that are contrary to our Muslim religion—things that are not true. He may even lead some people astray and make Christians of them. We must drive him away!" So when John was walking about the town, they would sometimes throw stones at him and say bad things to him. But John did not get angry, and he did not run away. He was a brave and kind man.

When Sa'eed saw how his teacher acted, he was surprised. He said to himself, "I am a true believer in God, for I follow the religion of Islam. This man John is an unbeliever, because he does not accept the prophet Muhammad. Now a believer should act better than an unbeliever, but really John is a better man than I am. For if anyone hits me, I hit him back. If anyone says bad things to me, I will say bad things to him in reply. We Muslims have thrown stones at John and have said bad things to him, but he did not get angry. Instead, he is kind to us. Why does he act like this?" Sa'eed did not yet know that it was Jesus Christ who had taught John to be kind to his enemies when they were unkind to him.

More and more Sa'eed came to admire his teacher John. He also liked the Bible they read together in Persian. Often he would go to John's little room to talk to him and to ask questions about the Christian religion. But Sa'eed's older brother Kaka did not want him to be a friend of the Christian. "Don't go to see this man any more," he said to Sa'eed, "for I am afraid you will one day become a Christian!" So for a time Sa'eed stayed away from John, and then he went back again to see his friend. He was really seeking to know the truth about God, and nothing could stop him. One day Kaka took his gun and was about to shoot Sa'eed, but God did not let him kill his brother.

When Sa'eed saw that his life was in danger because he liked the Christian teaching, he decided to leave his home. In the night he took his books and a few clothes and started off for Hamadan, where there were American missionaries and a Christian hospital. There he taught Persian to the missionaries, and the missionary doctor taught him how to care for the sick people. He also studied the Bible with the minister, and later he was baptized. How happy he was when his brother Kaka, who had once wanted to kill him, followed his example and became a Christian! Later Kaka became an evangelist, and

Sa'eed became a doctor. Both these brothers served Christ faithfully for many years in Iran.

Once, after Dr. Sa'eed had become a famous doctor, the governor in Senna, who was sick, sent for him and begged him to come and make him well. Friends advised Dr. Sa'eed not to go to Senna, for his enemies there still remembered him, and they might try to kill him. But the brave doctor, after asking God to show him what he should do, decided to go. He was able to help the governor get well, and he treated many other sick people, taking no money for his services. He also went to another distant place and operated on the eye of a great man in that region who was blind. The operation was successful, and the man was able to see again. As he was returning from his journey, enemies gave money to a bandit to murder the doctor on the road. But God guided him to travel another way, and he reached his home and family in Hamadan in safety.

Some years later, when Dr. Sa'eed was living in Teheran, he used to teach the Bible to friends who came to his home. One day while he was busy giving a Bible lesson, a man who had a painful boil on his neck entered the room and asked the doctor to treat it. Dr. Sa'eed asked the man to wait till he had finished the lesson. Then he went out of the room to get his instruments to treat the boil. After he left the room, the man said to the others in the room, "You don't know me. Many years ago I was hired to kill this doctor while he was on a journey in Kurdistan. Now I and my family of twenty-five people are in Teheran, kept here by the government. When we are sick, Dr. Sa'eed takes care of all of us and never charges us anything for his services." Truly he had learned from his master to love those who hated him, as Christ commanded: "Love your enemies, do good to those who hate you" (Luke 6:27).

Once I went to the town of Damghan. Every day I used to go about the streets and into the bazaar with Christian books in my hands, trying to sell them at a cheap price to all who wanted to read them. One morning I saw three men coming toward me, and I went to meet them. I said to them, "Gentlemen, *Salaam!* I have brought from Teheran some books I would like to show you. This book has some of the teaching of Jesus Christ, and this little book was written by Dr. Sa'eed of Kurdistan."

"Dr. Sa'eed!" exclaimed one of the men. "He saved my life."

"How was that?" I asked.

"I was very sick," the man replied, "and I went to all the doctors. I took all their medicines, but instead of getting better, I got worse. At last one of my friends said to me, 'Why don't you go to Dr. Sa'eed? He will pray for you and will give you medicine, and you will surely get well.' So I did that. I went to Dr. Sa'eed's office in Teheran, and when I sat down in his waiting room, I saw written in large letters on the wall these words: COME UNTO ME, ALL YE THAT LABOR AND ARE HEAVY LADEN, AND I WILL GIVE YOU REST. When I read those words, I said to myself, 'Here is where I get well!' Yes, the kind doctor prayed for me and gave me medicine, and I got well. He saved my life!"

"Thank God for that!" I said. "Now look at my books. Here is a little book in which Dr. Sa'eed tells how a sinner can be saved from sin by Jesus Christ. And here is the book in which those words you saw on the doctor's wall are written. It was Jesus Christ who said: 'Come unto me, all who labor and are heavy laden, and I will give you rest' " (Matt. 11:28). The men gave me the price of the books, took them from my hand, and went on their way. I never saw them again. But I hope they read the little books and believed in Jesus Christ.

Though Dr. Sa'eed had enemies who many times tried to harm him, God protected him, and he lived to be an old man. Most of the people who knew him, whether they were Muslims or Jews or Christians, loved and admired him because he was so good and was always kind to people who were poor and sick.

Dr. Sa'eed was never afraid or ashamed to tell people that it was Jesus Christ who had changed him and made him a child of God. On his tombstone in the Christian cemetery in Hamadan this verse from the Bible is engraved: I am not ashamed of the gospel: it is the power of God for salvation for everyone who has faith.

BIBLE READING: MATTHEW 5:43—48

13

How Merat Was Saved by Jesus Christ

In the year 1912, at a time when Iran was a weak country unable to defend itself, an army from Russia came to Tabriz and occupied the city. They arrested some of the important people and killed them, and they intended to kill also the chief of police, whose title was *Merat-us-Sultan* (mirror of the monarch). But Merat heard of their plan and fled on foot from the city. After traveling about twenty miles, he came to a village in which Armenian Christians lived, and the kind priest of the church took Merat into his own home and kept him safe during the long, cold winter.

When spring came, Merat decided he must go farther away, lest the Russian soldiers find him and kill him. When he thanked his host for his kindness and told him good-bye, the priest said to him, "Ever since you came to my home I have been praying to Jesus Christ to save you from your enemies and bring you safely to your family in Teheran. I am sure he will do this. When he does, will you remember that it was Christ who saved you, and will you promise to obey and serve him?" Merat was Muslim, but he promised to do what the priest asked. Then he fled out of Iran to Turkey, and after a long time he returned to his native land.

When he was nearing Teheran, the Russian soldiers arrested him one night while he was asleep and took him to Kazvin and put him in prison. There he was kept for some time, and he did not know what was going to happen to him. Finally a Russian colonel came to his cell and told him that the next morning at nine o'clock he would be taken out and killed.

Merat was terribly disturbed by this news, for he wasn't ready to die. He did not know that Jesus Christ had died for us sinners, that we might have eternal life with him. So he prayed to God, and he called on his prophet Muhammad, and all the other holy men whose names he knew, to save him from death. Finally, he remembered the Armenian priest and what he said to him about Christ. So he cried out, "O Christ, I am about to be put to death for something I did not do. This is not right. I beg you to save me!" After he made this prayer, he had peace in his heart, and he slept till morning.

Just at nine o'clock the Russian colonel came into Merat's cell and said, "Come with me!" When he came out of the prison and into the street, he saw a lot of Russian soldiers and crowds of men and women from Kazvin who had gathered to see what would happen to Merat. Many of the women were crying, because they did not want to see an Iranian officer put to death in his own land by foreigners. As Merat walked along the street guarded by soldiers, it seemed to him he was in a dream. He felt sure he was about to be killed by the Russians.

Suddenly Merat saw before him an officer and some soldiers in the uniform of Iran. When they came up to the Russian colonel, they stopped and gave him a letter, which he took and read. At once he took hold of Merat's hand and put it in the hand of the Iranian officer, and he and the Russian soldiers turned about and went away. Then the Iranian officer took Merat with him, and after a time they came to the Kazvin police headquarters and entered.

Merat thought he was about to be put to death, but it was a comfort to him that he would die at the hands of his own people, and not of the Russians. When he started to write a message for his wife in Teheran and asked the Iranian officer to send it to her after his death, the officer said with great surprise, "How mistaken you are! You are *not* going to be killed! Don't you know what has happened? A telegram came from the Russian embassy in Teheran, telling the Russians here to turn you over to the Iranian officers. That was the message I gave to the Russian colonel this morning. Now you are free; you can go to Teheran whenever you want."

At first this news seemed too good to believe. Then Merat knelt down and gave thanks to God for saving him in this wonderful way from certain death. And as soon as he was able, he started out in a carriage drawn by four horses to travel the one hundred miles to his home. How thrilled he was to see his wife and children again! But he forgot the promise he made to the Armenian priest to believe and to obey Jesus Christ, the one who had saved him.

One day a man named Nozad, a former friend of Merat who had become a Christian, met him on the street and said to him, "When you were in prison in Kazvin I also was there, telling the people about Jesus Christ. When I heard that your life was in great danger, I prayed much for you in the name of Christ. Now that you have been saved, do you realize that you are indebted to Christ for your safety?"

"Yes," said Merat. "Please tell me what I should do."

"You must believe in Jesus Christ as your Savior from sin," replied Nozad, "that your sins may be forgiven. Tomorrow I will take you to our church."

Next day Merat went with Nozad to the church where several American missionaries lived and worked. There he saw Iranian men gathered for Bible study and prayer, and he joined the group. When they knelt down to pray, Merat fell on his knees and said, "O God, forgive me for forgetting my promise to the Armenian priest! I know that it was Jesus Christ who saved me from death, and now I confess my faith in him." The other Christian men gathered around Merat and put their hands on his head and prayed for him, and when he arose, he was a Christian. How full of joy he was that Christ had saved him not only from death in Kazvin but also from all his sins!

However, there was something that troubled Merat very much, and that was the problem of his wife. He loved her, but he was afraid that if she knew he had become a Christian she might not want to live with him any longer. For, in the Muslim religion, it is not permitted for a Muslim woman to be the wife of a man who is not a Muslim. For a time Merat did not dare to tell his wife that he had believed in Christ as his Savior, lest she should say, "If you are a Christian, I will leave you!" While he was thinking how to tell her, she one day said to him, "There is something between us that I must tell you. While you were away in prison, I was sad, and I sometimes went to the church to pray and to get comfort. There I came to know Christ, and I believed in him. I am a Christian. Do with me whatever you want." She thought her husband might divorce her for giving up Islam!

Merat was overcome with joy to hear what his wife said. But he also felt ashamed of himself that he had not had as much courage as his wife in saying she was a Christian. How wonderful it was that God had led them both to faith in Christ! Now they could have a Christian home. So, in due time, the husband and wife and all their children were baptized and became members of the church in Teheran.

It was Merat's desire to serve the one who had saved him, so he accepted a position as business manager of the mission hospital in Teheran. There he had many opportunities to talk to the sick people and their friends about his Savior. He also was an elder in the church, and he often preached in the Sunday services. He became one of the leaders in the Presbyterian church in Iran.

One evening my wife and I were invited to the home of Merat and his wife for dinner. As we sat talking, I noticed hanging on the wall the picture of a stern-looking man in uniform. Then on the other wall was the picture of a man with a kind and smiling face.

"Whose pictures are these?" I asked.

"Both are pictures of me," replied Merat. "The first is my picture when I was an officer before I became a Christian. The second is a picture of me after Christ saved me. Do you see the difference?"

Indeed I did see the difference! Christ had made Merat a new man, a child of God.

BIBLE READING: ACTS 12:6—11

14

ROSTAM, THE HAPPY MAN

We all like happy people, don't we? Now I want to tell you the story of a man I knew in Teheran whose name was Rostam, and he was always so happy that his friends called him "Happy Rostam." Rostam was not a Muslim, as were the others whose stories I have told you. He belonged to a Zoroastrian family, and as a boy he followed the religion of his ancestors. Zoroaster was a great religious teacher who lived in Iran hundreds of years before Christ was born. He taught the people that there were two great Beings in the universe, a good Being and a bad Being. He said that people should obey the good Being and should fight against the bad Being. To do this they should have good thoughts, speak good words, and do good deeds. Most of the people of Iran followed the religion of Zoroaster before the time when the Muslims conquered their country, about six hundred years after the death of Jesus Christ. Then Islam became the official religion. Most of the Zoroastrians gradually became Muslims. However, some of them did not want to change their religion, and their descendants are still living in Iran and India. Rostam was one of them.

Not far from his home in Teheran there was a Christian mission school, the principal of which was Dr. Samuel Jordan. Rostam's parents sent him to this school. There he learned English as well as Persian, and he studied the Bible and learned about Jesus Christ. Mrs. Jordan was eager for the boys in the school to love and follow Christ, and she formed a little group, which she called the Brotherhood, to which boys who wanted to know Christ better were invited. Rostam became a member of the Brotherhood.

In 1923, I came from Meshed to Teheran on my way to America. I was asked by Mrs. Jordan to speak to the boys in the Brotherhood at their weekly meeting. I did so, and I told them about my journey to the Afghan border and my talk with the Muslim man as we traveled along the road (see chapter 6). You remember how I told this man that Jesus Christ is the Way and the Light and the Bread of Life and the giver of the Water of Life and that anyone who has faith in him can make the journey of life safely. I didn't know at the time whether any of the boys who heard this story were influenced by it to follow Christ. But long afterward, Rostam told me that when he heard in that little meeting that Jesus is the Way, the Light, and the Bread and Water of Life, he believed in him. When he did so, God filled his heart with joy and gladness. Later he was baptized in the name of Christ and became a member of the church in Teheran. Dr. Sa'eed was of great help to Rostam as a teacher of the Bible and a loving friend.

After Rostam graduated from the mission school, he and about twenty-five other young men from Iran who knew English were chosen in 1925 to go to Detroit to study in Henry Ford's school. They were to learn all about the Ford cars and then to return to Iran to be Ford's agents in selling his cars. While he was in Detroit, Rostam was taken into the home of a minister who was kind to him. He also attended the church and the meetings of the young people, and he was as happy as could be.

But, sad to say, Rostam became sick. He could not walk or do his work, so he had to go back to Iran. Lying on a stretcher, he traveled by trains and ships, for at that time there were no planes that flew to Iran. It was a long journey, and he was alone, but he reached his home in safety. He told us that the doctors in America informed him that he would not live long. But he replied to them, "I know that Jesus Christ will not let me die so soon!"

"How were you able to make that long journey on a stretcher alone?" we asked.

"Oh, it was not difficult," he replied, "for everywhere Jesus Christ raised up friends for me who helped me along." No doubt Rostam's happy spirit made people glad to be of help to him.

After his return to Teheran, Rostam began to get better, and soon he was able to walk again. Dr. Jordan gave him a job in the library of the mission school, and he was glad he could be with his friends once more. But after a time he again became weak and could no longer walk. His home was on the street along which the boys would walk as they went each day to school. So when the weather was good, Rostam's mother would help him go out of the house and sit in a chair at the door. Then he could greet his friends as they passed by, going to and coming back from school.

Rostam used to say to his old friends, "We aren't Arabs, we are Iranians. We should not say *Salaam* to one another, for that is an Arabic greeting. Instead, we should say *Shadzee* [which means "live happily"]. And for good-bye we should say *Shad Bash* ["be happy"]." Those are Persian words. So when his friends passed him, Rostam always called to them, *"Shadzee!"* and they in reply said *"Shadzee"* to him.

If you had seen this young man at that time, you might have thought that he would be sad, not glad. Not only was he unable to walk, he was unable to see well. He talked slowly, and his hands trembled so much that it was hard for him to shake hands with anyone. He could not even feed himself, and his mother had to put food into his mouth. His friends who went to America with him all had good jobs with plenty of money, and he was poor and unable to work. But it seemed that the worse his condition became, the greater was his joy. Once he said to me, speaking slowly, "I am so glad I am weak like this, for if I had not become like this, I would never have known the love of God." What a wonderful spirit he had!

Rostam's greatest joy was going to church every Sunday. Two of the young men from the church would hire a carriage and take it to the door of his house. Then they would help him into it, and when they reached the church they would carry him inside. There he would sit on a back seat during the service. To be in God's house with his Christian friends was indeed like heaven to him.

His friends in Detroit wrote Rostam many letters, and this greatly pleased him. Once when they sent him a generous gift of money, he decided he would use a part of it to have a party for the members of his church. This he did, and, sitting at the door of the church hall, he greeted each one with a hearty *"Shadzee!"* After his friends had drunk tea and eaten the cakes he had provided, some of the young people carried Rostam to the front of the room and seated him on a chair facing all the people. Then they put a garland of flowers around his neck and crowned him as the Angel of Gladness. That was a day Rostam never forgot.

You may have learned in school that the Greeks had a hero named Hercules who was very strong. The people of Iran also have an ancient hero who was said to be very, very strong, and his name was Rostam. Our friend happy Rostam was named for this hero. When our Rostam became so weak in body, he used to say with a laugh that the hero Rostam was a physical champion but that he was a spiritual champion! Indeed he was, for he had overcome discouragement and sickness by his strong faith in Christ and his joyous spirit.

The people of Iran love poetry, and many of them write verses just for fun. Rostam made up some poems about himself and his spiritual victories. Once when he had a calling card printed to give to his friends, he had his name printed as Shad Rostam Shademan (happy Rostam ever happy), and under his name he put this little verse that he had written:

In old Iran a mighty man was Rostam;
The least of all, Rostam the happy man, I am.

Many people forgot that his name was Rostam and called him Shadzee.

It is difficult to translate poetry from one language to another, for it often loses much of its beauty in the process. However, I will try to put one of Rostam's poems into English for you:

A man of Iran is Shadzee,
 Made happy by God our Father.
Happy indeed is Rostam,
 Who in place of "Good-bye" says "Shad Bash."
Did you see any kindness in Rostam?
 That's from God's love without doubt.
The doctors all said, "There's no hope,
 This man will never get well."
But my hope is ever in Jesus,
 And in him I am always joyful.
Do you ask how I keep on living?
 By the love of my God in Christ!
So now you know my condition,
 And why I'm in love with Jesus.

While Rostam's body became weaker and weaker, his spirit remained strong and joyous. Finally he said to his mother and brothers, "I am soon to go to be with Jesus Christ. When I die, do not weep for me, but tell my brothers in the church to have a joyous celebration for my going to be with Christ." On Thanksgiving Day in 1939, Rostam died. Soon after that a joyous service was held in the church, at which Dr. Jordan and other Christians spoke. They remembered and thanked God for Rostam's wonderful spirit.

Happy Rostam was indeed, as a friend said, "a mighty man of Christian joy and victorious living." Truly, in God's sight he was a greater hero than the great champion for whom he was named.

In another brief poem Rostam explained what it was that made him so joyous:

> Jesus was crucified to save us from sin,
>> Ever in us for comfort God's Spirit has been.
> Shadzee! Our Savior ascended on high!
>> That is why "Shad Bash" is our Persian good-bye.

BIBLE READING: JOHN 15:9—11

15

How Jalily
Became Joyful

I told you about Rostam, who, even when he was sick and weak and poor, was always happy. At this time that he was rejoicing in Christ, there was in Teheran another man who was not happy. His name was Jalily. He was not an invalid like Rostam; he was able to walk to his office every day. He was not poor, for he had a good position with the government. He had a good education, for he had been taught by private tutors in the court of the Shah, where he had lived when he was a child. He had a wife and children. He lived a good life and followed the teachings of his Muslim religion. But still he had no joy, for it seemed to him that something was lacking in his life. Sometimes he used to get up early in the morning and pray to God to give him what he lacked to make him a joyful person.

Jalily had a son named Jahangir whom he loved and to whom he wanted to give the best education possible. So he sent Jahangir to the mission school where Rostam had studied, of which Dr. Jordan was the beloved principal. There the boy learned English as well as Persian, and he studied the Bible and learned about Jesus.

One day when Jahangir returned home from school, he brought a little card to his father. "My dear father," he said, "Dr. Jordan sent this card to you." Jalily took the card and read the Persian message printed on it. It was an invitation to come to the church where meetings would be held every night for a week. Jalily had never been to the church, so he did not know what was done in church meetings. But he had high regard for Dr. Jordan and was grateful for the good teaching that his son was getting in the Christian school. So he at once said to Jahangir, "Since Dr. Jordan has invited us, I will, of course, accept his kind invitation, and you will go to the church with me tonight."

That evening father and son walked together from their home to the church—the same church in which Rostam loved to praise God. When they entered, there were many people there who had arrived before them. They found vacant seats and sat down, and Jalily was wondering what would be done in this meeting.

Soon the organ began to play, and all the people who were able to read opened the hymnbooks and sang a Persian hymn. Some knew the tune, and some, like Jalily, did not; but all tried their best to follow the organ. This music greatly pleased Jalily, for when he was a boy he had some lessons in playing an instrument called a *tar*, which was something like a guitar. Then the minister prayed to God. The prayer also pleased Jalily. The Muslim prayers that he prayed three times every day facing Mecca were in Arabic, a foreign language. But this Christian prayer was in his native tongue, which everybody present could understand. However, he wondered why these Christians closed their eyes during the prayer, for in the Muslim prayers people always kept their eyes open.

After the prayer there was more singing, and then the minister read some verses from the *Injil* (the New Testament). Jalily had always heard about the *Injil* of Jesus, but he had not read it. So he was glad to hear what it said and to be able to understand it, for it was read in the Persian translation, about which I have told you. He had always read his holy book the Koran in Arabic, which he sometimes did not understand too well. "That is right," he said to himself. "Surely God's Word should be read in the language that people can understand, not in some foreign tongue."

Then the minister began to talk. The title of his sermon was "Sin and Salvation." He told the people how Adam and Eve, our first parents, had disobeyed God by eating the fruit in the Garden of Eden. This disobedience was sin. As a result of their sin, Adam and Eve were put out of the garden, and they later died. Ever since then, every one of their descendants—except Jesus Christ alone—has inherited a sinful nature from them and, like Adam and Eve, disobeys God's commands. A baby may look pure and good, but before long it will begin to disobey its parents and do many things that God does not like, because it has the root of sin in its heart.

When Jalily heard this, he was much surprised. He knew that people who killed others and who stole what did not

belong to them and who got drunk were sinners, but he had thought that since he did none of those evil things he was not a sinner. Now God opened his eyes to see that he, too, had disobeyed God many times; so he, too, was a sinner who needed salvation.

The minister also said that God had shown his great love to us sinners by sending a Savior, his own Son, Jesus Christ. Jesus loved us so much that he died in our place on the cross, that we might be forgiven and saved from sin. Jalily had always heard from his Muslim teachers that Jesus was not God's Son and that he did not die on the cross. But as he listened to the sermon, God made it plain to him that what the minister said was true. Yes, there was a Savior greater than all the prophets—greater than Muhammad—who loved us so much that he gave his life for us. What wonderful love was his! And Jesus not only died for us, but also he came to life again. And he is alive today, able to save us from sin and sadness and make us truly joyful.

When the meeting ended, the minister said to the people, "If any of you want to come to Christ to be forgiven and saved from your sins, please take a seat at the front of the church." Most of the audience went out, but a number remained and came forward and sat down on the front benches. Among those who remained were Jalily and Jahangir. The minister then said, "Sin is a disease. When anyone gets a disease, he goes to a doctor who knows how to cure that sickness. Who is the doctor who is able to cure the terrible disease of sin? There is only one who can do this. He is Jesus Christ, who died for us, and who is alive among us now. Just as a sick man goes to a doctor in whom he trusts, puts himself in his hands, and does what the doctor tells him to do, so a sinner can come to Jesus Christ and trust himself to this Savior. Christ never rejects anyone who comes to him. He will forgive us, cure us, and help us to live pure and good lives."

When Jalily heard this, he and Jahangir stood up, and he said, "When I came into this meeting, I thought I was the best person here, but now I know I am the worst. I am a sinner, and now I believe in Jesus Christ and ask him to save me. I will follow and serve him as long as I live." Other people also said the same.

Jalily later used to say, "When I left the church that night, I felt that a heavy burden had been lifted from my heart. I was happier than I had ever been in my life. When I reached home, my wife was surprised to see me so happy. She asked what had happened to me. I told her I had become a Christian." Later the whole family was baptized.

Jalily faithfully kept his promise to serve Christ to the end of his life. When his Muslim friends in his office asked him why he had left their religion and had become a Christian, he invited them to come to his home. There he gave them a warm welcome, served them tea and cakes, and told them how Christ had saved him from sin and had given him lasting joy. Later he began to hold a little meeting in his own home every week to which he invited his friends. They would drink tea together, for in Iran tea is always served to guests. Then they would read the Bible, and often they would sing Christian songs. And Jalily would lovingly invite those who were not Christians to believe in his Savior. Some of them did so.

After Jalily finished his work for the government, he studied in a Bible school and graduated at the age of seventy. Then he became an evangelist of the church. Many journeys he made to distant cities to sell Christian books and to tell people about Christ. I had the great privilege of being with him on some of these journeys. He was always so kind and so humble that people usually treated him with great respect. "Jalily is a real Christian," they often said.

Once when Jalily was in Tabriz, where he had been born, he tried to find his relatives whom he had not seen for many years. But they were not at all happy when he told them he was a Christian. However, a young man there who was studying to be a doctor came to see Jalily and became his friend. He said that the people he met never smiled at him or showed any love to him. But he had seen in the face of Jalily  the joy and love he so much wanted. He was drawn to Jalily as iron is drawn to a magnet. What was this love that drew him? It was the love of Christ that shone so brightly in the face and in the life of this man of God. The young man, too, became a Christian.

Bible reading: Matthew 11:28—30

16

BEHZAD AND HIS BEAUTIFUL PAINTINGS

I know you like to draw pictures, don't you? You may even dream of becoming an artist when you grow up and of painting beautiful landscapes or portraits. Now I want to tell you about a friend of mine who was a famous artist in Teheran. His name was Hussein Behzad.

I first saw Behzad one night in the church in Teheran. There had been a meeting in the church to which Muslims and Jews, as well as Christians, were invited. The minister told the people how Jesus Christ had come from heaven to save us from our sins and to make us children of God, and he invited everybody to believe in this Savior. When the meeting came to an end and the minister had said the final prayer, most of the people left the church. Then one of the Christian men came to me and said, "I have brought my friend Behzad here tonight, and he is sitting at the back of the church. He needs Jesus Christ very much. Please come and meet him!"

So I went to the back of the church, and there I saw a little man who looked very unhappy. It was Behzad. He was an artist, and he was able to paint beautiful pictures. But, sad to say, his own life was not beautiful, for Behzad had acquired a few bad habits. He was using opium and alcohol, and he had become sick and weak, and he was not able to quit these habits. He was really a slave bound by these evil chains, and he could not get free. Naturally he was sad and hopeless.

Behzad's Iranian friend told him that Jesus Christ had the power to set him free, and he urged him to believe in Christ and be saved. Previously both of them were Muslims. After they had studied the Bible and had understood who Jesus is and what he has done and will do for us, they were baptized and became members of the church in Teheran. With the help of Christ, Behzad was able for many years to continue his painting, and he became known as the best miniature artist in Iran.

As you know, some artists paint big pictures. But the miniature artists of Iran paint small pictures. The flowers or animals or faces of people are drawn in such detail that a magnifying glass is needed to see them clearly. And how is the artist able to paint things so small? He, too, uses a magnifying glass, and he uses a brush that may have only one or two hairs to draw the tiny lines. I used to visit Behzad and his wife to pray for them and to talk with them about Jesus Christ, and I often saw him at work. He always sat on the floor with his legs crossed under him as he painted his pictures on a low table beside him.

After he became a Christian, Behzad painted a little picture of Jesus Christ and gave it to me. I have it before me now as I write this story. It represents our Lord surrounded by clouds of glory, and there is a halo of light about his head. Under the clouds are written these words in the beautiful Persian script:

Master of Love, Lord of truth,
    Savior of all, Christ the Lord.

And he signed the picture "Servant of Christ, Behzad." How happy I was to receive this lovely gift from my friend! After that Behzad painted a number of Bible pictures for me and for other friends.

There was at that time an organization in New York called Lit-Lit, which intended to teach people who had never gone to school how to read and write (this is literacy) and to prepare books for them in a language they could read (this is literature). Now you see why it was called Lit-Lit. The people who did this work hoped that many of those who learned how to read would read the Bible and believe in Jesus Christ.

In order to get money for printing books, every year Lit-Lit sold many thousands of Christmas cards. They asked Christian artists in all lands to paint the best pictures they could about the birth of Christ and to send them to New York, where the best of all the pictures they received would be chosen for the Christmas card of the year. Behzad's missionary friends in Iran heard about this and urged him to enter the contest. He did so, and he painted a beautiful picture of the wise men bringing their gifts to the baby Jesus, who is resting in the arms of his mother Mary. This picture won the prize, and in 1958 more than three hundred thousand of Behzad's cards were sold and sent to people all over the world by their friends. How happy we all were that Behazd was able in this way to serve his Savior!

To thank Behzad for this lovely picture, Lit-Lit sent him a citation and a special medal made for him. Three of his Christian friends in Teheran went to his little home to present them to him. He was at work in his studio, sitting on the floor as usual. He stood up. And when the medal was presented and words of appreciation were spoken, Behzad replied, "I have received many honors in my life, but I prize this honor more than any of the others. For the other honors came to me from men, but this has come from Jesus Christ."

Behazd did something else for which I was grateful. I am sure you know that when missionaries leave their native land and go to other countries to serve Jesus Christ, people in the churches from which they go often give the money that is needed for their travel and for their living expenses in their new homes. For many years the members of the Calvin Presbyterian Church in Philadelphia gave the money for my support in Iran. They also prayed for me and wrote letters to me and encouraged me in doing God's work. Not only the grown-ups but also the children in the Sunday school helped to support me by their gifts, and the different classes sent me cards at Christmas, signed by all the children. So, of course, I greatly appreciated all that the people of Calvin Church did for me.

Once when I was planning to come to America for a visit, I wanted to bring a nice gift to Calvin Church to show my gratitude. What could I bring? As you know, Iran is famous for its Persian rugs, so I decided to take to the church a rug woven in Iran. But instead of an ordinary rug to be put on the floor, I wanted to take one with a picture of Christ woven into it to be hung on the wall. Where could I get such a rug? Of course it could not be bought in the bazaar.

I had a friend in the town of Semnan named Bagher who was a master rug weaver. He had married the daughter of Gasem (chapter 3), and he, too, had become a Christian. Once when I was a guest in their home, I asked Bagher if he could weave a rug for me to give to the church that would have in it a picture of Christ. "Yes," he replied, "I can do that. But you must get someone to draw the pattern for me. I can't weave it without a pattern."

Have you ever looked closely at a Persian rug? If so, you noticed that it was made up of thousands of little knots of wool thread of different colors tied onto strong white cotton cords. From the pattern the weaver knows how many knots of each color he must tie in each row to form the picture. When he follows the pattern carefully, the picture will come out beautifully. It takes a long time to weave a good rug, for every separate knot is tied by hand.

When Bagher said he needed a pattern, at once I thought of Behzad. "Do you think Behzad could prepare a pattern for you?" I asked.

"Oh, yes," he replied. "No one could do it as well as Behzad."

When I returned to Teheran, I went to see Behzad. I asked him if he would make a pattern in which there would be a picture of Christ. At once he agreed to do this, and he chose as the subject Martha kneeling before Christ as he was about to raise her brother Lazarus from the grave. You can read the whole story in the eleventh chapter of John. When Behzad finished drawing the pattern, he brought it to me, and I wish you could have seen it—it was a beautiful picture of Christ!

Then I took it to Semnan to Bagher, and he went to work weaving the little rug. He took many weeks to finish it, for he worked on it only in the evening after his other work was over. When at last I saw the finished rug, I was delighted, for it was a thing of beauty, with its bright colors of red and blue and green and yellow. I was sure the Calvin people would love it.

When I reached America and was invited by the pastor of Calvin Church to speak on Sunday morning, I took the rug with me and hid it behind the pulpit. When I spoke, I told the people how Behzad and Bagher had become Christians and how they had used their wonderful talents to make a rug in which was woven a picture of Christ. Then suddenly I lifted the rug from behind the pulpit and held it up for all of them to see. So surprised and so thrilled were the people by the beauty of this work of art that a murmur of "Oh" went up from the congregation. They did indeed love this gift from Iran. They made a frame for it and put glass over it to keep it safe and clean. Today it is hanging on the wall of the church for people to admire. I wish you could see it!

The picture in the rug reminds us that Jesus Christ, who gave physical life to Lazarus after he had been dead and buried for four days, is able to give spiritual life also to people like Behzad, who are captives of sin. Christ gives them new hearts and makes them happy and strong to serve God. If Christ had not given this new life to Behzad, he would never have painted all those beautiful pictures, which have brought joy to so many people.

BIBLE READING: JOHN 11:21—27

17
THE GARDEN
OF GOOD NEWS

What grows in a garden? Well, if it's a vegetable garden, all sorts of things good to eat grow in it—such as peas and beans and tomatoes and potatoes and corn. And if it's a flower garden, all sorts of lovely flowers good to see and to smell grow in it—such as roses and sweet peas and violets and nasturtiums and chrysanthemums. (What big names some flowers have!) But I know of a garden where something else grows besides beautiful flowers and trees. This is a garden in which Christians grow! Now let me tell you about it.

Teheran, the capital of Iran, which I have mentioned so often to you, is a big city situated in a huge plain. If you stand in one of the big avenues of Teheran, with your right hand to the east where the sun rises and your left hand to the west where the sun sets, your face will be to the north. And what will you see? You will see a high range of mountains running east and west, which for many months of the year wears a white cap of snow. This range is called the Alborz Mountains. Just before you, about ten miles from Teheran, rises the mountain called Towchal, which is fourteen thousand feet high (that is nearly two miles higher than Teheran).

If you should ride in a car from the city toward the mountains, you will find that the road becomes rather steep. And then, when it reaches the foot of the mountains, it stops! If you want to go farther up the mountain, you will have to ride a donkey or walk. It would take you many hours to climb to the top of Towchal, where you might have a snowball fight in June! These mountains have no trees on them, except in the narrow valleys along the streams that flow down from the melting snow.

In summer Teheran often becomes very hot, and many people used to go up for their vacations to the region near the foot of the mountains where the weather is delightfully cool. Many gardens were there, around each of which were high walls to keep out thieves and wild animals. In these were shade trees and flowers and pools of water. In these lovely gardens grownups could sit and talk and read, and children could play all day long. In some of the gardens there were houses in which the people could sleep at night, but often they would sleep under big tents. Usually they ate their meals sitting under the trees. And if they wanted to take hikes, there were the great mountains ready for them just outside the gardens.

One of these beautiful cool gardens was used for their summer vacations by several of the missionary families in Teheran, and what happy times we all had together! Our family always slept in a big tent, but we spent the rest of the time under the trees or walking about on the mountainside. The children learned to swim in the pools from which the gardener used to get water to sprinkle on the flowers every afternoon.

When the children grew up and went to America for their education, we wondered what we could do with the garden. How could it be used in God's work in Iran? Just then the Presbyterian church in Iran decided that it was necessary to train some members of the church to tell Muslims and Jews the good news of Jesus Christ, so that they too might believe in him and be saved from sin. When I was asked to arrange a course of study and to teach the students, I thought that the best place to have this school was our garden. It would be a summer school, and the students could live together as a big family. They could have their lessons and eat their meals in the open air, and they could sleep in the two buildings that were in the garden. The school began in June 1948 with about a dozen students. The big tent in which our family used to sleep became the chapel of the school.

You have probably heard that another word for Good News is *evangel*. From that word we get a longer word, *evangelism,* which means telling the good news of Christ to people who have not believed in him; one who tells the Good News is an evangelist. So our little school was called the School of Evangelism, and the garden in which the school was conducted became known as the Garden of Evangelism, the place where evangelists were trained.

What did the students learn in this school? They learned the Bible in the Persian language; they learned how Christians had taken the good news of Christ to all parts of the world; and they learned how to explain to Muslims and Jews the truths that Christians believe. They learned also how to pray and how to lead a meeting and how to deliver a talk. And they also learned how to keep their rooms tidy, how to wait on the table, and how to wash the dishes. They learned, too, how to live together in peace and love and how to forgive one another. Perhaps this was the hardest lesson of all!

Who were the students who came to the Garden of Evangelism? Some were fathers and mothers, the oldest of whom was Jalily, whose story I told you. He graduated when he was about seventy years old. Also there were boys and girls in their teens. Many were Armenians and Assyrians, whose ancestors became Christians several hundred years after the birth of Christ. Others came from Jewish and Muslim families and had only recently become Christians. All came to this school because they wanted to learn how to be better Christians in order to serve Christ well in Iran. Sometimes one of the young students would say, "When I came here, I thought I was a Christian. But really I was not a Christian, for I had never given my life to Christ and I had not been born again by the Holy Spirit. Now I have believed in Christ and have become a real Christian."

In the afternoon after lessons were over and we had had our tea together, the younger students usually played volleyball. That is a good game that all can take part in. But once a week we used to go out all together for a walk up the mountainside. There was a high hill to which we used to climb, and there we would rest. However, some of the strong boys and girls would climb up a steep place to what they called the Three Rocks. They would stand up on them and shout to us far below. Then they would run down the mountain like deer and be ready for the picnic supper of bread and hard-boiled eggs and cucumbers that we had brought with us.

By the time supper was ended, the sun would have set. Then we would sit on the hilltop looking down on the great city of Teheran, ten miles to the south and far below us. We would watch the lights come on all over the city, indeed a wonderful sight. And before going back to our garden we would have our evening prayers, when everyone would make a brief prayer. We always thanked God for the beautiful mountains rising up behind us to the sky. And we prayed for the millions of people before us down in Teheran who did not know Christ. Their city was bright with thousands of lights, but many of their hearts were dark; only Christ the Light of the world could make them bright. After the prayers, we would sing a hymn, perhaps "The Light of the World Is Jesus," which we all loved. Then we would go down the mountain, often slipping and sliding in steep places in the darkness. And we would rejoice and have a prayer of thanksgiving to God when we all arrived back in the garden safe and sound.

Now I want to tell you about one of the students who came to the School of Evangelism for three summers and, having spent the required nine months in study, received a certificate of graduation. Mehdi was born in Isfahan. One day when he was a little boy in the first grade of school, he went with a relative to the big mission hospital in Isfahan. There someone gave to the little boy a little blue book. With great joy, Mehdi took the book to his home and showed it to his mother. The title of the little book was *God Has Spoken,* and it had in it many verses from the Bible. It was in Persian, but Mehdi did not yet know how to read very well, so he hadn't read his book. But he loved it, for the blue cover was pretty.

However, when his mother saw the book, she became angry. "You can't have this book," she said to Mehdi, "for this is a book of the Christians, and you must not read it!" You see, his family members were all Muslims, and they thought the books of the Christians were not true. So his mother snatched the book away from the boy and hid it, and he didn't know what she had done with it. How sad was little Mehdi to lose his pretty blue book!

Some years later, when his family was moving its things, what should appear in a pile of old papers but the little blue book! Mehdi grabbed it and kept it safe. By this time he was able to read well, so he eagerly read what God had spoken, and he knew it was all true and good. Now he loved the book more than ever.

After a while he went to Teheran, and one day he walked past the reading room of the church. In a show window by the sidewalk he saw some books, one of which was open. He read a little of it, and there in this book were the same words of God that he had read in his little blue book. So he went inside. There Jalily met him and put in his hand a copy of the book he had seen in the window. It was the Holy Bible. How eagerly Mehdi read it! He began coming to the Bible class that met every night in the reading room, and before long he believed in Jesus Christ.

When his family learned that Mehdi had become a Christian, they were angry and told him he could never come home again. So he got a job as a helper in a hospital in Teheran; and whenever he had time, he came to the Bible class and to the church services. Later he was baptized. He felt so grateful for what Jesus Christ had done for him that he decided to become an evangelist, and so he came to study in the Garden of Evangelism. After he got his certificate, he traveled far and wide, giving people books about Christ, similar to the little blue book that had led him to Christ, and telling them about his Savior.

What grows in the Garden of Evangelism? Christian men and women who are serving Christ in Iran today. The fruit of that garden is good.

BIBLE READING: MATTHEW 13:31—32

18

THE LADY WHO LOVED THE CHILDREN

Once upon a time there was in Pennsylvania a little girl named Leree Chase. Leree went to Sunday school and to the services in her church. She also read her Bible and learned how much Jesus loved her. She loved Jesus, too. When she was ten years old, she gave her heart to him. That is the most important thing any girl or boy can do.

When you love someone, you want to do something to please that person and to show him how much you love him. Leree loved Jesus so much that she decided she would go to people who did not know him and would tell them about him and would show them his love. Jesus, you remember, told his followers to go into all the world and to tell the good news of his salvation to everybody. As you know, people who go to tell the good news of Christ to others are often called missionaries. Leree made up her mind that she would become a missionary. So she studied hard in school and later in college; she learned all she could to be ready to serve her Lord well.

Some missionaries serve Christ in needy places in their own countries. Others go to foreign lands, where people speak different languages and follow different religions. They are sometimes called foreign missionaries. When Leree finished college, she became a foreign missionary and went one third of the way around the earth to the country of Iran to serve Jesus Christ. The first thing she had to do after she arrived in Teheran was to learn to speak and to read the Persian language. She first learned little sentences like *"Een dast-i-man ast"* ("This is my hand"). Then she learned stories about Jesus that she could tell to the people she was going to meet.

Miss Chase had her home near the homes of other missionaries from America in the big city of Teheran. But she had always hoped to spend her life helping the poor people who lived in hundreds of little villages not far from Teheran. Most of the village people at that time had no schools; they could not read a book or even sign their own names. Many of them did not have good homes to live in or good food to eat. And they had never heard how Jesus loved them and came to save them from sin and bring them close to God. Of course, many changes have come to Iran in recent years, and the life of the people in the villages is much better than it used to be. But even now most of the people of Iran do not know and follow Jesus Christ.

After Miss Chase learned the Persian language, she sometimes went out of the city and traveled from village to village, telling the women and children about Jesus and his love. There were no good roads to the villages, and no cars, so she and her friends would ride on little donkeys. I'm sure you would have liked that, wouldn't you? In every village kind people would invite them to stay in their houses. When the women and children came to see who this foreign woman was, Miss Chase told them about Jesus and his love for everybody. And the people all loved Miss Chase because she was so good and kind.

Then in 1939 the Second World War began, and two years later foreign armies came into Iran. Many of the rich people who had stores of wheat would not sell it, hoping that later they could get more money for it. So many of the poor people had no food to eat, and crowds of villagers poured into Teheran seeking bread. But there also food was very scarce. There were no empty houses in Teheran in which these people from the villages could live. So they dug holes in the ground and made little huts for themselves to get some protection from the rain and snow and cold of winter. I am sure you never saw anyone as poor as these villagers.

Now that so many village people had come to Teheran, Miss Chase did not need to ride a donkey out to the country to see them. Instead, she could get in a carriage drawn by a horse and ride in it to the part of the city where the poor people had settled. But what could she do to help them? She did not have money to buy bread for them. However, her heart was full of the love of Jesus Christ, and so she found a way to show that love to some of them.

One day she went to the poor section of Teheran. There she rented a small room not far from the place where the villagers were living. Then she took there some pieces of nice white cloth on which she had drawn pictures of flowers. She also took some colored thread—red and blue and green—and some needles. When several little girls came to the room to see what this lady was doing, Miss Chase taught them to embroider—how to sew flowers on cloth with threads of different colors. This was the first time that these children had ever seen anything really white and clean and beautiful, for they were too poor to have nice clean clothes to wear. So they loved to come to the sewing classes and to hear the stories of Jesus that Miss Chase told them each week. And they loved their kind teacher. Many of them learned how to make lovely tablecloths and towels, which Miss Chase sold for them. This money helped them buy food for themselves and their families.

One day a little girl with a bright face whom I will call Fatima (this was not her real name) came to the sewing class. Because it was a cold winter day and Fatima had no coat, Miss Chase said to her as she was leaving, "Fatima, here is a nice warm coat I will give you to keep you warm." The little girl was happy and ran off to her home, proud of her pretty coat. But when she came back the next week she did not have her coat. "Fatima," said Miss Chase, "where is your coat?"

"Oh, my father sold it to buy opium," replied Fatima. Sad to say, both her father and her mother took opium, a drug that makes people weak and lazy. So, instead of working, Fatima's parents sat by the side of the street and begged people to give them money. Then they used the money not for food for their child, but for more opium. They even sold her coat to get money for their opium.

Miss Chase felt so sorry for the poor little girl who was hungry and cold that she said to Fatima's mother, "Will you let me take your daughter to my house? I will feed and clothe her, and I will send her to school."

"Yes," said the mother, "I can't care for her. You take her." So Fatima went to Miss Chase's home, where several other girls like her were living with Miss Chase as her daughters. There she had good food to eat and warm clothes to wear and more love than she had ever before had in her life. And Miss Chase sent her to the Christian school nearby. Fatima had never gone to school, but she worked hard; and at the end of the year she had the best grades in her class. Miss Chase taught her about Jesus and his love for children, and Fatima believed in him and gave her heart to him. She became a Christian.

For about nine years Fatima lived with Miss Chase and her other girls. Then she went away to Meshed to be trained as a nurse in the Christian hospital, about which I told you (chapters 2 and 4). After she had become a nurse, she returned to Teheran and got a job in a large government hospital. It was in this hospital that the Crown Prince, the son of the Shah of Iran, had been born not long before Fatima began to work there. She was the only Christian nurse in the hospital, for all the others were Muslims.

One day the brother of the Shah brought his wife to this hospital to have a baby. Three nurses were assigned to care for the princess, one of whom was Fatima. The baby arrived safely, and the mother and child were about to return to the palace. But the nurse who was to come from England to take care of them in the palace had not yet arrived. So the brother of the Shah said to the superintendent of nurses, "I want one of your nurses to go with us to the palace to care for my wife and baby till the English nurse arrives."

"Very well, sir," said the superintendent. "Which of the three nurses who were with you here do you want?"

"We want Fatima," he replied. "She is the best nurse." So Fatima went with the prince and princess and baby to the palace.

When Sunday came, Fatima went to the prince and said, "Sir, may I have some time off from work today?"

"Why do you want time off?" he inquired. "This is not a holiday." In Iran, Friday is the weekly holiday, and people usually work on Sunday.

"Sir, I want time off so I can go to church," she said.

"Oh, no," replied the prince. "You can't have time off today. You don't need to go to church. You are not a Christian, for your name is a Muslim name. No, you must work today!"

"But, sir," protested Fatima, "I *am* a Christian, and all that I have has come to me from Jesus Christ. On Sunday, I must go to church to thank him for all he has done for me!"

When the hour of service in the church arrived, a car from the palace, driven by one of the royal chauffeurs, came to the church door, and Fatima got out and went into the church to worship with Miss Chase and her old friends while the car waited for her outside. After the service she hurried to the door to get into the car and return to the palace. But her friends ran after her, saying, "Stop, Fatima, tell us what it's like in the palace!"

"No, I can't stop now," said the nurse. "I must hurry back to my work. I will tell you later."

So she jumped into the royal car and returned to the palace. There she remained till the nurse from England arrived. Then she went back to her hospital in the city.

How did it happen that a poor little girl from the slums became a fine nurse and was able to help the family of the Shah and to tell them that she was a Christian? It was because the love of Christ in the heart of Miss Leree Chase poured into Fatima's heart and life and made her a Christian, ready and eager to serve her Savior wherever she was—either in the palace or among the poor in the hospital.

BIBLE READING: MATTHEW 25:31—40

19

How a Schoolboy Found the Truth

I told you the story of a man named Hasan who was born in the city of Meshed in the eastern part of Iran (chapter 10). There are many men and boys in Iran whose first name is Hasan, who were named for the grandson of Muhammad. Now I want to tell you about another Hasan, who lived in the province of Mazanderan near the Caspian Sea in the north of Iran. How different this region is from most parts of Iran! The central part of the country is a high plateau, or tableland, where little rain falls and crops and trees need irrigation. But along the Caspian Sea there is a great deal of rainfall; the country is green and beautiful, and the mountainsides are covered with forests.

Hasan lived in a little town on the shore of the sea. He liked to watch the fishermen as they went out in their boats to drop their long dragnets into the water. Then how exciting it was to see them pull the nets up onto the shore and take out the shiny fish that had gotten caught in them! But, much as Hasan liked to watch the fishing, he liked even more to go to school and to learn all he could from books. His teacher was a kind man whose name was Seyd Musa. *Musa* is the Persian for Moses, and *seyd* is a title used in Iran for people who are descended from Muhammad. But Seyd Musa was not a Muslim. For, through a missionary named Dr. Schuler, he had learned about Jesus Christ and had become a Christian.

One day Seyd Musa said to his pupil Hasan, "Do you want to know the truth about God and salvation? If so, you should study the Holy Bible and the Koran and compare the two books. If you do this, you will find the truth." At once Hasan began to do what his teacher had suggested, for he was eager to find the truth about God.

Seyd Musa gave Hasan a copy of the Persian Bible, and he found this book easy to read, for it was in his mother tongue, and it was interesting. He also had a copy of the Koran, which, as I told you (chapter 1), is the holy book of the Muslims. But reading this book was not easy, for it was in the Arabic language. Hasan had studied Arabic in school with his teacher, but it was a foreign language to him. It was as strange to him as Latin or French might be to you. At that time Muslims usually thought it wrong to translate the Arabic Koran into other languages; they said it should be read in Arabic. However, Hasan was able to understand its meaning and to make notes on its teachings. He did the same for the Bible. Then he arranged his notes in two columns: "What the Bible Says" and "What the Koran Says." It took him a long time to finish this task. When it was completed, he read his notes with great care and compared the teachings of the two books. Then he concluded that the truth was in the Bible, not in the Koran, and he believed in Jesus Christ.

Dr. Schuler lived in Teheran, but now and then he would go to Mazanderan to tell the people there about Christ. He would ride on horseback over the high mountains that rise up like a wall between the capital and the Caspian Sea. Once when he visited Seyd Musa, he was happy to see Hasan and to learn that he, too, had become a Christian. The young man asked to be baptized, and Dr. Schuler gladly baptized him. Hasan and his teacher were the only people in that region who had left Islam and had become Christians.

After several years, Hasan decided to find a wife for himself and to get married. Of course, a Christian should marry a Christian and establish a Christian home, in which father and mother and children would all love and serve Christ together. But there were no Christian girls in Hasan's town, so he married a nice Muslim girl. He told her he was a Christian and invited her to become a Christian also. She said she wanted to remain a Muslim, but she did not object to her husband's following Jesus Christ. Later, when children were born to them, they were baptized by Dr. Schuler and other ministers who came from Teheran to visit them.

After Dr. Schuler left Iran and went to California to live, I made a journey from Teheran to the Caspian Sea. I didn't travel on horseback as the early missionaries had done, for cars were then running on the road that had been built over the mountains. I rode in a bus. When I went to Hasan's home to call on him, I was sorry to learn that his wife had been ill and was still sick in bed. I was taken to her room to speak to her and to

pray for her, and she said to me, "A wonderful thing happened to me!"

"What was that?" I asked.

She replied, "When I was very sick and the doctors thought I was going to die, Jesus Christ came to me and said to me, 'You will get well; I have healed you.' From that day I began to get better, and now I am almost well. I will soon be up again."

"That is indeed wonderful!" I said. "Now tell me: what do you think of Jesus Christ?"

"He is, of course, the Savior," she replied, "for he saved me from death."

"Do you believe in him as your Savior from sin?" I asked. "And do you want to be baptized, as your husband and children have been?"

"Of course I do," she said. So in due time she was baptized, and the family became a Christian family.

I remembered that Hasan had been baptized long before by Dr. Schuler, and I knew that Dr. Schuler would be happy to hear that Hasan's wife also had become a Christian. So I wrote to him to tell him the good news. Soon I received a reply from California. Dr. Schuler wrote, "I am happy to hear that Hasan's wife has become a Christian, for I prayed for her for twenty years."

At that time Hasan kept a shop in his hometown in which he sold groceries and all sorts of things that people need in their homes. But he was such a faithful follower of Christ that some of his Christian friends thought he ought to leave this work and to spend his whole time in telling the good news of Christ to other people. So when the School of Evangelism of which I have told you was established, Hasan became one of the students. How happy he was to be able to study the Bible with a teacher and to learn the things that would help him to become a good evangelist!

After he received his certificate from the school, he and his family left their hometown and went to serve Christ up on the plateau, first in Hamadan and then in Teheran. In Teheran, Hasan became known as Shapur. There he had charge of the Christian reading room. Every day he and Jalily would welcome the men who came to read the Christian books. They would tell them about Jesus and his love for all people. And every night he conducted a Bible class there, to which Christian and Muslim young men came to study God's Word. Some of the Muslims in this class believed in Christ.

People who live in Teheran and other cities in Iran where there are Christian churches are able, if they wish, to study the Bible in classes like the one in the reading room. But what about the people who live in towns in which there is no church and no Christian teacher? Someone had the idea that these people might study the Bible by correspondence. How would they do this? Well, to anyone who asked for it, a copy of the gospel of Matthew in Persian would be sent by mail, and with it several questions on the first chapter. When the answers to those questions had been sent back by mail and a grade given to the student, questions on the second chapter would be sent. In this way people far from any

1. William M. Miller, *Ten Muslims Meet Christ* (Grand Rapids: Eerdmans, 1969).

church were able to learn much about God's Word and the good news of Christ. I think you would have had fun studying the Bible by correspondence!

In Teheran, this Bible correspondence work was given to Shapur. Because he loved to write letters, he was able to help many people with their difficulties. One man might write to him and say, "The Koran says that Jesus was not the Son of God, but in the book you sent me it is stated that Jesus is the Son of God. Do you Christians think God took a wife and had a son?" Or another might write, "The holy Koran says that Jesus did not die on the cross but was taken alive by God to heaven. Why do you Christians say that he was crucified and died on the cross?" Often others would say in their letters that they knew Jesus had told his disciples that Muhammad was coming and that they should believe in him. "Why, then," they would ask, "do the Christians not believe in Muhammad?"

How good it was that Shapur had studied the Koran and the Bible carefully. He was able to explain these difficult matters to the Muslims who inquired. He always wrote to them with understanding and love, and so he was able to tell the good news of Christ with his pen as well as with his tongue.

BIBLE READING: MATTHEW 1:16—20

20

How Mulla Abbas Was Changed

There are thousands of towns and villages in Iran in which there is no church, and in many of them there is not a single Christian. But God loves the people in these places, and he wants them to know that he has sent his Son, Jesus Christ, to save them. Of course, they will never know what God has done for them unless someone tells them or gives them books that explain how they may be saved from sin. Most of the missionaries who have gone from Europe and America to serve Christ in Iran have made their homes in the large cities, where they established schools and hospitals and churches. But a few of them, like Miss Chase and Dr. Schuler, often made journeys to other smaller cities and even to the villages to tell to the people the good news of Christ.

One of the towns to which missionaries in Teheran sometimes went was Damghan, situated about 250 miles east of

Teheran, on the road to Meshed. I mentioned this town in the story of Dr. Sa'eed (chapter 12). The houses of Damghan were made mostly of sun-dried brick, like the adobe houses in New Mexico. And the narrow streets were dusty in summer and muddy in winter. So Damghan was not a pretty place. But God loved the people who lived there, and he put it into the heart of the Reverend Ivan Wilson to go there and to show his love to them. Mr. Wilson was sure that there were people in this little town who would believe in Christ if they heard the Good News.

It was not always easy for missionaries to visit these small towns, for sometimes the police officers mistakenly thought they were spies of some foreign nation and would order them to leave. Once the police in Damghan forbade Mr. Wilson to bring Christian books there, and they sent him back to Teheran. But later he returned, and this time he was able to go about the streets selling Bibles and other Christian books. Whenever anyone showed enough interest to buy a book, Mr. Wilson would say, "Wouldn't you like to come to see me in my room? I am staying in the guesthouse. Come and have a cup of tea with me!" He hoped and prayed that some who really wanted to know and follow Christ would visit him.

One evening a guest did come to call on him. His name was Abbas Rahabi. From seeing the white turban he wore on his head, Mr. Wilson at once knew that his guest was a mulla, a teacher of the Muslim religion. The missionary welcomed him warmly and poured him a cup of tea, and they began to talk. Soon, however, it became clear to Mr. Wilson that Mulla Abbas had not come to learn more about Christ. Not at all! His purpose was to argue with the missionary and prove to him that his teaching was false and that Islam was the true religion.

Mr. Wilson tried to tell his guest how God loved the people of the world so much that he sent his Son to die for us and to save us from our sins. But Mulla Abbas rejected all that the missionary said. "No," he protested. "The holy Koran, which is the Word of God, says that Jesus is *not* the Son of God; he is God's prophet. And the Koran says that Jesus did *not* die on the cross, for we believe that God took him alive to heaven. And the Koran also says that Jesus told his disciples that Muhammad, God's last and greatest prophet, was going to come, and that they must all believe in him. Then why have you Christians not accepted the prophet Muhammad and become Muslims? God will punish all who reject his last and greatest prophet!"

When Mr. Wilson tried to explain to Mulla Abbas that Jesus Christ was greater than any of the prophets, that he really died on the cross, came to life again after three days, and is still alive, and that he did not say that Muhammad was coming but promised that he himself would be with his followers always, the Muslim teacher would not agree. Try as he would, Mr. Wilson was unable to convince him that the Bible is a true book. "No," said the mulla. "This book of yours is not God's Word, for it says things that are contrary to what the Koran says. This is a book you Christians have written yourselves, and what it says about Jesus is false."

Mulla Abbas thought he had defeated the missionary in this argument, and he was feeling proud of himself. Then he looked at Mr. Wilson and saw a strange sight: the tears were pouring down the cheeks of the missionary. Mr. Wilson was so deeply hurt that Abbas rejected Jesus Christ, and he felt so sorry for him in his unbelief that he began to cry.

Several years passed. Mr. Wilson returned to America, and other missionaries went to Damghan. Then I visited this town. While I was there, a Communion service was held in my room in the guesthouse. Only two people were present: one was the missionary, and the other was Mulla Abbas! We ate the bread and drank from the cup, as Jesus commanded his disciples to do in memory of him. Then we prayed together and thanked God for sending his Son to save us. It was a lovely service, and Christ himself was present with us. For he promised that wherever even two or three of his disciples met together in his name, he would be present.

I had never seen Mulla Abbas before, so after our prayer I said to him, "My dear brother, I never heard what it was that led you to Christ and made you a Christian. Will you please tell me?"

Abbas, with deep feeling in his voice, replied, "It was Mr. Wilson's tears that led me to Christ!"

"How strange!" I said. "Please tell me how that happened."

Abbas replied, "You know Mr. Wilson. He came here to tell the good news of Christ, and I decided to visit him and to argue with him and to prove that Islam is the true religion. Mr. Wilson tried hard to convince me that the only Savior is Jesus Christ. But I answered all his arguments and felt proud that I had defeated this Christian missionary. And then Mr. Wilson began to weep. His great heart was grieved because of my pride and unbelief. And his tears did for me what his arguments did not do. They melted my hard heart, and I believed in Christ." Mr. Wilson had truly shown God's love to this proud Muslim teacher.

On my next journey to Damghan, a meeting was held in the home of Abbas, with his wife and six children all present. We sat in a circle on the floor and read the Bible and prayed together. Then I had the joy of baptizing his whole family. They became a Christian family, and through them other people in Damghan became Christians. But Abbas was not well. His eyesight was failing, and when he wanted to write a letter, he would dictate it to his small son Mehdi, who in this way learned to write very well. Once Abbas and Mehdi came to a meeting of Christians in the Garden of Evangelism, and what a happy time they had with their Christian brothers! The father said he hoped his son would become an evangelist.

Not long after that, Abbas became quite sick and died, and his home was broken up. The youngest girl, Manijeh, was taken by Miss Chase to her home in Teheran and became one of her daughters. She was sent to school and later to college in Beirut, to prepare for the service of Christ. Her brother Mehdi Rahabi also came to Teheran, received a certificate from the School of Evangelism, and after serving as an evangelist for several years, went to India for more theological training. Then he returned to become one of the leaders in the church in Iran.

All this happened because a Christian man, whose heart was full of the Spirit of God, made a missionary journey to Damghan. There he had so much love for a proud Muslim mulla that he wept over his lost condition. It is love like this that God uses to bring people to himself.

Bible reading: Colossians 3:12—14

21
GOD'S LIGHT DISPELS DARKNESS

The man whose story I am going to tell you now was named Norollah by his parents, which means "light of God." But if you had met this man when he was a young doctor in Teheran, you would not have seen any light or joy in his face; for at that time he had not known Jesus Christ, who is the true Light of God.

Norollah studied medicine in Teheran and became a doctor. He knew that the American Mission Hospital had good doctors and nurses, who treated thousands of the sick people of Teheran and other cities every year. So he asked Dr. Hoffman, who at that time was the head of the hospital, if he could work with him. (This was the same Dr. Hoffman whom we previously met in Meshed in chapters 2, 4, and 11.) He felt sure that in this hospital he would learn much from the experienced

American doctors and that he would also be able to treat many people who had all kinds of diseases. Dr. Hoffman accepted the young doctor, and for some time Dr. Norollah helped in the care of the sick people. He loved his work, and he learned much, but he was really not happy.

There was always a question in his mind that he could not answer: Why did these American doctors love their work so much? And why were they so happy in it? He had seen other doctors who didn't love their work and who treated the sick people not so much to help them as to get all the money from them that they could—and these doctors were not happy people. Why was there this difference between Dr. Hoffman and Dr. Cook—the missionary doctors—and other doctors he knew? Dr. Norollah finally decided it was because these doctors from America were skillful and were able to make many people well that they were so happy. Also, they had nice homes and a good living, and it seemed they had nothing to worry about. So Dr. Norollah determined to become the head doctor of a hospital and to make lots of money. He was sure that he, too, would then be happy. He didn't know how small were the salaries that the missionary doctors received.

Dr. Hoffman realized that his assistant was not happy. So one day he said to him, "Dr. Norollah, may I ask you what your religion is?" Of course, Dr. Hoffman knew that the young man came from a Muslim family. But since he never said the prayers facing Mecca, as every Muslim should do, and because he did not keep the fast of Ramadan for twenty-eight days every year, it seemed as though he did not place any importance on his religion.

Dr. Norollah didn't want anyone to talk to him about religion, and he replied, "Don't ask me about religion! I have no religion except the practice of medicine." So Dr. Hoffman was not able to tell his unhappy friend about Jesus Christ, the Light of the world, who is able to shine into dark and troubled hearts and make them bright and joyful.

When Dr. Norollah left the mission hospital, he married, and two sweet little daughters were born to him. He became the head doctor in a hospital. He charged his patients high fees, and in this way he became rich. He had gotten all the things that he thought would make him happy. But after ten years he realized that he still was not happy. So what was it that made these American doctors happy? He thought perhaps it was the climate of America. He would go to America and see for himself!

His friends in Teheran said to Dr. Norollah, "Don't go to America! You don't know English well, and you will not be admitted into a medical school—the language of which is English. You know the French language; why not go to France and study there?"

"No," replied Dr. Norollah. "I must go to America and find the secret of happiness." His wife had become mentally ill and had to stay in a hospital. So he sold his medical practice to another doctor, took his two daughters with him, and went off to America. He knew no one in America, and he didn't know where to go. But a Christian friend of Dr. Hoffman advised him to go to Boston and said to him, "It would be good for you to attend church services. Ministers in the churches speak good English, and you and your daughters could learn much from them."

In Boston, Dr. Norollah began to go to a church to improve his English. The pastor, Dr. Bradley, was a good speaker, and the doctor and his girls were always present in Sunday school and in the Sunday services, as well as in prayer meeting on Wednesday nights. They liked Dr. Bradley and the church. They learned some English, and they also learned a good deal about Jesus Christ and the Christian religion.

However, one night in the prayer meeting Dr. Bradley said something that Dr. Norollah did not like. He said that many people think that money and fame and success and pleasure will make them happy, but they are mistaken. Only Jesus Christ is able to make one truly happy. When Dr. Norollah heard this, he said to himself, "Dr. Bradley is talking just at me. He shouldn't do that!" When the meeting was over and the people were speaking to their minister at the door, Dr. Norollah was so angry that he would not speak to Dr. Bradley, and he walked quickly past him into the street.

Then that night the doctor had a wonderful dream. When he awoke in the morning, he was surprised to find himself happier than he had ever been before. No longer did he want to be rich or famous; he wanted only to serve God and help other people. How did this happiness that he had sought for years come to him so suddenly in Boston? He did not know, but he felt sure it had somehow come to him through the church and through Christ, as the minister had said. So he at once went to see Dr. Bradley to apologize for not having spoken to him the night before. He told the minister, "I know it is Christ who has given me the happiness I sought, so I have believed in him. My daughters and I want to be Christians." Before long Dr. Bradley baptized all three of them.

Life then became different for the doctor and his girls. They were happy in their school, and their father was admitted to a medical college for further study. The future looked bright. But then Dr. Norollah began to think about his friends in Teheran who were just as unhappy as he had once been. He had found the secret of happiness. It was not the climate of America, or money, or success; rather, it was faith in Christ, who gives lasting joy (John 15:11). So he decided he must go back to Teheran and tell his friends that they didn't need to go to America to become happy, for Christ would make them happy just where they were. So back to Teheran he and his daughters went.

One morning as I was sitting in my room, there was a knock at the door, and in came Dr. Norollah, his face beaming with love and joy. He introduced himself to me, and then he told me his story, much as I have told it to you. "See what change has come into my face!" he exclaimed. "For ten years I had such a dark, ugly look in my face that I was ashamed to have my picture taken. I looked like a criminal! Now you can see that the frown has all gone and that the joy that is in my heart is shining from my face." And indeed it was!

When his old friends saw him, they said, "What has changed you? Have you brought a fortune back with you from America?

"No," replied the doctor. "I found something better than that. Christ has made me truly happy!" When they heard his story, several of them also said they wanted to become Christians. Once a week these friends used to gather in the doctor's little home to read the Bible and to pray together, and I usually met with them.

One night a young man whom I had not seen before was in the meeting and told us why he was there. He said, "Last week in the middle of the night my old mother became very sick. I wanted to bring a doctor to see her, but I was afraid to ask anyone to come, for our doctors won't go out of their houses at night unless one first puts a large sum of money into their hands. I did not have a lot of money, so I didn't know what to do.

"Then I remembered that I had heard that Dr. Norollah had come back from America and that he had changed; he was not charging his patients as much as he used to. So I went to his door and knocked—but really I was afraid of what he would say to me for waking him up from his sleep. However, there was no need for fear! He came smiling to the door, and he said he would go at once with me to see my mother.

"When I asked timidly how much he would charge, he replied, 'I don't work for money anymore; I work for God. You can give me whatever you want.' I had never heard a doctor talk like that! But he spoke the truth. He went with me, and he gave good treatment to my mother, and she recovered. And he accepted with gratitude the small sum I was able to give him. Truly Dr. Norollah has been changed by Christ, and I, too, want to become a Christian."

Thereafter, whenever people would praise Dr. Norollah for being such a good and kind doctor and for making them well, he would reply, "It is not I; it is Christ who healed you. I prayed to him, and he told me what to do for you. You should thank him, and believe in him." Jesus once said to his disciples, "You are the light of the world." Truly Dr. Norollah showed the light of God's love to many people who were in darkness.

BIBLE READING: MATTHEW 5:14—16

22
THE GIRL WHO FELL INTO THE FIRE

O nce upon a time there lived in a village in the mountains of Iran a little girl named Zahra.* Zahra's home was very different from your nice home. The walls of her house were made of mud, and there were no windows. The floor was dirt, and there was no carpet. When Zahra's mother wanted to cook dinner, she made a fire in a hole in the dirt floor in the middle of the room, and the smoke went up around the walls and out a hole in the ceiling. So Zahra's home was not clean and pretty. But Zahra was a happy girl, especially when her little friends came to play with her.

One day, when two of her friends came to see her and the three of them were romping about the room, a terrible thing happened: Zahra stumbled and fell into the fire that was in the

*This is not her real name.

middle of the room, and her dress caught fire. She didn't know what to do, so she ran to the door to find her father, who was outside. By the time her father had picked her up in his arms and put out the fire, Zahra was terribly burned. Her neck, her chest, and her body were all burned.

If anyone should get burned in your home, there are doctors and nurses and hospitals not far away to take care of him. But in Zahra's little village there was no doctor or nurse, and there was no medicine for burns. What could be done for Zahra? There was nothing her parents could do for her except put some rags on her burns and hope they would heal. The burns on her neck did heal, but in a way that made her chin stick to her chest, so that she could not raise her head easily. The other burns did not heal, and Zahra was getting weaker and weaker.

One day a neighbor came to Zahra's father, whose name was Hosein,* and said to him, "You *must* take Zahra to see a doctor, for if you don't, she may die!"

"I know," said Hosein sadly. "But where is a doctor?"

"There are many doctors in the city," replied the neighbor. "Do take Zahra to one of the doctors in Resht!" (You can find Resht on your map near the Caspian Sea.)

"No," said Hosein, "I can't do that, for the doctors there charge too much money. I am a poor man; I have no money to pay a doctor!"

"But I have heard," replied the neighbor, "that there is an American doctor in Resht who has a hospital. They say that he is a good doctor and that he is kind to poor people; and he

*This is not his real name.

151

does not take much money from them. Take Zahra to the American hospital! I hope God will heal her there."

"Very well," replied Hosein, "I will do as you say." So early next morning Hosein wrapped his little girl in a cloth and held her gently in his arms as he rode on his donkey down the trail from his village. At that time there was no road for cars to this village. So Hosein guided his little donkey down the mountainside, and then away across the plain. After a long time they reached the city. There Hosein asked people where the American hospital was, and they told him where to go. At last he stopped in front of a big door, above which was written in large letters in the Persian language AMERICAN CHRISTIAN HOSPITAL. Hosein got off his donkey, carried his little girl inside, and put her down.

How did it happen that in Resht, on the other side of the world from America, there was an American hospital? It was because Christian people in America long ago sent some missionary doctors and nurses there to heal the sick people and to tell them of Jesus and his love for everybody. So Zahra was taken to a Christian hospital. Soon the doctor came and looked at the little girl, and he said to her father, "She is in a bad way, but we will do all we can for her. And we will hope that God will heal her." Then Hosein got on the donkey and went back to the village. And Miss Degner, a kind nurse, carried Zahra upstairs and bathed her and put her in a nice little bed with white sheets. This was the first time in her life that Zahra had slept in a bed, for in her home she had always slept on a mattress on the floor.

Next day, the doctor put Zahra to sleep and began to treat her burns. When she awoke, she felt a lot of pain; but after a few days she became more comfortable. The nurses were all kind to her, and a few nice people brought her flowers for her room and toys to play with. Christians from the little church brought her some pretty pictures of Jesus, and they sang songs to her about Jesus and his love. But after a time the doctor again put her to sleep and operated on her burns to get skin to grow over them. He had to do this many times. And during all this painful time of treatment, Zahra didn't want anyone to touch her except Miss Degner, the missionary nurse, who was so gentle and loving. Zahra stayed in the Christian hospital for a whole year.

At last the doctor one day examined all her burns, and said to her, "Zahra, you are well; you can now go home!" If you had been in a hospital for a whole year, and the doctor one day said to you, "You are well; you can go home," wouldn't you be happy! But what do you think Zahra said? "I don't want to go home. I want to stay here," she said to the doctor.

"Oh, no," said the doctor. "You are well, and you must go to your home." So he sent for her father. Zahra's father came with the donkey, and he took Zahra up the mountain to her home. Of course, her mother and all the neighbors and friends were glad to see the little girl again, with her burns healed. But Zahra wasn't happy, and she began to cry. "I want to go back to the hospital!" she wailed. Her father couldn't stand to hear his little girl cry so much, so he put her on the donkey and took her back to the hospital. When the doctor saw her, he said, "Zahra, why have you come back?"

"Because I like it here, and I want to stay here," she replied.

Then Miss Degner came and said, "Didn't I tell you, Zahra, that you can't have that bed any longer? That bed is for a sick child, and you are well now."

But Zahra insisted that she did not want to go home. So Miss Degner sent for Miss Winkelman. She, too, was a missionary nurse, but she did not work in the hospital. In her own home in the city she had a clinic to which poor mothers brought their babies, and Miss Winkelman taught them how to bathe them. She also often gave them milk when they were too poor to buy milk for the babies. She used to tell these mothers how much Jesus loves the poor people and the little children. When Miss Winkelman came in, Miss Degner said to her, "Would you be able to take Zahra to your home and care for her as your little girl? She says she doesn't want to stay in her own home in the village."

"Yes," replied Miss Winkelman. "I will care for Zahra." Miss Winkelman already had two little girls about the size of Zahra, whom she was caring for as her daughters. So when Zahra went to live with her, instead of having two girls, who looked like twins, Miss Winkelman had three little girls, who looked like triplets!

Zahra went to school and learned to read. If she had stayed in her village, she would never have learned to read and write, for there was no school in that village at that time. Every Sunday she came to Sunday school and to the church service with Miss Winkelman and the other girls, and there and in her home she learned about Jesus. And she did an important thing: she gave her heart to Jesus Christ and became a Christian. You see, her parents were not Christians. They were Muslims and followed Muhammad, instead of Jesus.

So everybody was happy—except Zahra's parents. They were not happy, for they were up in the village and Zahra was down in the city, and they could not see her as often as they wanted.

Then one day Hosein came to the hospital, leading the donkey. On the back of the donkey were piled all their possessions, which were some bedding and a few pots and pans. When the doctor saw Hosein, he said, "Why have you come? Is somebody sick?"

"No," replied Hosein. "But we got lonesome for Zahra, so we have come to the city to live so we can see her more often."

"Very well," said the doctor. "But what work will you do to earn money to care for your family?"

"Please give me some work in the hospital," said Hosein. "Let me help the nurses in taking care of the sick people, taking their food to them, and doing other things for them."

"All right," said the doctor. And he gave Hosein a long white coat to wear and sent him to the men's ward to work.

One day I went to the men's ward to tell the sick men who were lying there about Jesus and how he used to heal the people who were sick. When I entered, I saw that Hosein was talking to one of the men lying in bed, and I listened to hear what he was saying.

"Did you know that Jesus can make dead people alive?" Hosein asked.

"No," said the sick man. "How did you know that?"

"Because," replied Hosein, "he made Zahra alive."

"Who is Zahra?" asked the man.

"She is my little girl," replied Hosein. "She was dead, or almost dead, and Jesus made her alive again. So I know he can raise the dead to life."

Not very long after that, Hosein came to the pastor of the little church in Resht and said to him, "I have been a Muslim and have believed in Muhammad. But now I believe in Jesus, and I want to become a Christian."

"Very good," said the pastor. "But why do you want to become a Christian?"

"Because," replied Hosein, "Jesus can raise the dead to life, and I know he is the Savior. He made Zahra well, and now I want him to save me." So Hosein was instructed in the Christian faith, and later he was baptized. Both father and daughter became members of the Resht church. After some time, Zahra's mother and the other children also believed in Christ.

Zahra once said to me, "God has been so good to me, and Christian people have been so kind to me; I want to become a nurse and help people who are poor and needy, as the missionaries helped me."

BIBLE READING: MARK 5:22—24, 35—43

23

A Guest Is Knocking at the Door

The people of Iran love to have friends visit them, and they are rightly famous for their hospitality. When a guest comes to one of their homes—even though it may be a stranger—they always give him their best. If one is a guest in the home of rich people, he will be treated like a prince and will be fed the most delicious foods that the cook is able to prepare. And if he visits a poor home, there, too, will he be given the nicest things in the house. These hospitable people would rather give their choicest dainties to a guest than eat them themselves. They have a saying that a guest is a gift from God, and the hosts always thank a guest for taking the trouble to honor them by coming to their home. If anyone should be rude to a visitor or should shut the door in his face, he would be considered a bad person. How many people, poor and rich, received me into their homes with the greatest kindness during the many years that I was in Iran!

Once I was invited to visit Shiraz, the beautiful city in the south of Iran in which Henry Martyn translated the New Testament into Persian (chapter 8). Many years after Martyn's death, English missionaries went to Shiraz and established a fine hospital and a church. When the time came to build a place of worship for the church, the pastor, who was the Reverend R. N. Sharp, wanted to have a beautiful building that the people of Iran could admire and love. So it was built not like an English or American church; but, rather, like the mosques of Iran, with a domed roof and lovely tile work on the walls. The Christians of Shiraz are proud of their beautiful church in which they worship God.

I was asked to come to Teheran and to spend a week in Shiraz, to help in the evangelistic meetings that were to be held each night in the church. Of course, I was most happy to accept this invitation. Every night I talked about Jesus Christ and told the good news of salvation to the people who were present—many of whom were Muslims.

On the last night, I announced to the people that a wonderful guest had come and was even then standing at the door knocking. I said this guest had come from a distant place, from heaven. He is a great person, greater than any prophet or angel, for he is the Son of God. Though he is so great, he was willing to humble himself and to come to this earth to visit little people like us. As he now stands outside the door, he says, "Behold, I stand at the door and knock; if anyone hears my voice and opens the door, I will come in to him, and eat with him, and he with me."

If the master of the house comes to the door and opens it and welcomes this guest, what will he do? He will enter with love and will fill the house with his light. He will clean up the dirty rooms and make the house beautiful. Then he will sit down with those who received him and eat with them, and he will talk with them, and he will make them happy forever. But if those who live in the house should shut the door and refuse to receive him, he will patiently wait for a time. Then if the door is never opened for him to enter, he will go away sorrowing, leaving those inhospitable people alone in darkness.

I said that this guest is Jesus Christ, who wants to enter the door of our hearts and live with us forever. And I begged the people to open the door to let him in. Some of them said they would do so and would always love and obey Jesus Christ.

Next day I went to several homes in Shiraz where I had been a guest to say good-bye to my kind friends. One of these was the home of a lady known as Miss Ella, who had a school for girls. When I told her good-bye, one of her pupils was standing by her. This girl had lived in the home of Miss Ella for a number of years and had been treated like a daughter by her teacher. Since the girl was being brought up in a Christian home, I supposed that she also was a Christian. But to be sure I said to her, "You are a Christian, aren't you?"

"No," she replied, "I am not a Christian."

Then I said to her, "May I ask you a question? Suppose you were sitting in your room alone one evening, doing your homework, and you heard a knock at your door. When you went to the door and asked who was there, you heard the voice of your dear teacher Miss Ella saying to you, 'It is I, please open the door and let me in.' What would you do?"

"I would be very glad. I would open the door at once for her!" exclaimed the girl.

"Of course you would," I said. "Miss Ella has been so kind to you, I am sure you would not want to keep her waiting even for one minute. But is it not strange that you have not opened the door for another guest—one who loves you even more than Miss Ella does? You heard me tell last night how Jesus Christ has come to be your guest. Ever since you came here to live with Miss Ella, Jesus Christ has been standing at the door of your heart; and he is still knocking and waiting for you to open it and let him in.

"Jesus is your friend and your Savior. He loved you so much that he died to save you. He is alive and wants to come into your heart and to make you happy. I wonder why you have kept him waiting so long. If you would open the door so quickly for Miss Ella, why don't you do it for Jesus Christ?"

The girl looked down at the ground and made no reply. I said good-bye and went back to Teheran.

After some days the postman brought me a letter from Shiraz. When I opened it, I found it was from this girl, and I eagerly read it. It was written in Persian, and the translation is something like this:

My dear sir:
I write to tell you good news. I was not willing to keep that heavenly guest, Jesus Christ, waiting any longer outside the door. I have taken him into my heart, and I am now a Christian. I am happy, and I know you also will be happy to know that Jesus is my Savior.

And she signed her name. Indeed I was happy! And Christ also was happy that he had been welcomed into the heart of a sweet girl. For Christ loves young people and little children, just as he loves their fathers and mothers. He wants to enter every heart.

Do you know the little chorus:

Come into my heart, Lord Jesus,
Come in today,
Come in to stay,
Come into my heart, Lord Jesus.

I hope you will not only sing this but also receive the Lord Jesus as your guest and will love and serve him all your life.

When Jesus Christ is really living in our hearts, we want him to enter and live also in the hearts of our friends and in the hearts of all the people of the world. And we will do everything we can to make the good news of Christ known to everybody everywhere. It was for this that I went to Iran, and I am most grateful to God for calling me to serve him in that land as a missionary.

If God should tell you to go to some place where people do not know Christ and to spend your life in making him known and showing his love to them, you should obey with joy. For I know of nothing that you could do with your life that would be better than that. "For God so loved the world that he gave his only Son, that whoever believes in him should not perish but have eternal life" (John 3:16).

BIBLE READING: REVELATION 3:20

William McElwee Miller spent forty-three years as a missionary to Iran where he translated and prepared several books and Bible commentaries in Farsi. He is the author of *A Christian Response to Islam*.